MERLEAU-PONTY'S

CRITIQUE OF REASON

MERLEAU-PONTY'S

CRITIQUE OF REASON

by

THOMAS LANGAN

NEW HAVEN AND LONDON YALE UNIVERSITY PRESS 1966

Library of Congress catalog card number: 66–21525

ACKNOWLEDGMENTS

I WISH TO THANK Editions Gallimard for permission to quote from Merleau-Ponty's works, and Madame Maurice Merleau-Ponty for entrusting the manuscript of *Le Visible et l'invisible* to me for a prepublication reading of it. To Monsieur Jacques Vidal, Janine and I owe much more than a careful correction of the manuscript that kept him up until three in the morning, when the Boulevard Raspail is at last quiet. Rather, on our many month-long trips with him and Madame Vidal, we have learned the sense of many of the things written about in this book.

PREFACE

WHEN MAURICE MERLEAU-PONTY died recently at the age of 53 the shock went beyond the already great sorrow accompanying the premature silencing of a creative mind. Sartre, in the memorial issue of *Les Temps Modernes,* was moved to write one of the most sensitive and searching self-examinations in all literature, seeking (not altogether successfully) to understand what it was that had brought about his estrangement from the man who had been the moving spirit of that journal in its early years. Paul Ricoeur and Alphonse De Waelhens both wrote of a grave, irreplaceable loss. It was not just that of a vital *homme de gauche* (the title Jean Beaufret very justifiably chose for his memorial article in *L'Express*). That loss, admittedly, was itself catastrophic, for Merleau-Ponty had developed into one of the profoundest political critics of our time, devastating for doctrinaire Marxism and effectively disturbing to right-wing *grand bourgeois* politics.

But the reason Merleau-Ponty could be (like Ricoeur) a source of creative vision on the French Left is to be sought in his philosophy, indeed in his ontology. The prominence he enjoyed as philosopher, rivaling on the Continent Heidegger and Sartre, is owed to his having advanced creatively a great tradition in its seemingly necessary development one stride closer to fullest self-possession of its own implications. The sense of his ontology is revealed only to those willing to understand it as a development motivated by internal tensions of the tradition of transcendental philosophy flowing from Kant through Fichte and Hegel, which has given birth to Marx on the one hand and Kierkegaard and Nietzsche on the other, and in our time, has blossomed into the transcendental phenomenology of Edmund Husserl and the existential fundamental ontology of Martin Heidegger.

In the introductory chapter of this study I have sought to present a brief summary of these developments as they motivate Merleau-

Ponty's philosophy. There I explain what I take to be the inner tension of the whole tradition we shall call "transcendental philosophy." Those requiring a fuller review of these developments since Kant will find them in my section of *Recent Philosophy* and in the two-volume study of *The Phenomenological Movement* by Herbert Spiegelberg. In the chapters following, I have sought to bring out the sense of Merleau-Ponty's "fundamental ontology" (as Heidegger would term it) and to present it as an answer to those tensions which drove Kantianism to become Hegelianism and Hegelianism to become existentialism. In the final critical chapter it is argued that Merleau-Ponty did not succeed in relieving this tension and in solving the difficulty, but it is acknowledged that his profound development of the tradition has considerably clarified issues still obscure as late as Heidegger's postwar publications.

The chapter headings are not puns, and the organizational scheme they reveal is not an artificial device. I believe the analysis amply supports the contention that Merleau-Ponty's philosophy is a "critique of reason" and that the development from *The Phenomenology of Perception* through the political essays to the last writings on language and art do not merely parallel roughly the three Kantian Critiques, but rather the development they reveal is impelled by the same internal necessity implicit in both philosophers' transcendental starting point.

The critical analysis which follows can serve as a general introduction to Merleau-Ponty's philosophy. But given my end—to understand this thought as a development of a whole tradition and through it throw light on the central tension in that tradition—the present study does have a particular critical orientation. This deliberately results in two special characteristics. First, no effort is made to impress a public unaware of it with the immensity of Merleau-Ponty's contribution to the entire contemporary cultural scene, a contribution in fact staggering both for its breadth and its depth; at times, as for instance in his critique of behavioristic psychology, it is definitive. Fortunately, I have been able at least to suggest in passing all of the themes of these many contributions and something of their character. Fortunately again, English translations of all his works are now available, and Merleau-Ponty's French is not quite the insurmountable barrier Heidegger's German has proven. Second, this analysis is rather boldly systematized—boldly, but I trust not falsely. This is particularly the case in Chapter 5. What will appear to the reader who does not know Merleau-Ponty as mere paraphrase will strike the student of his works as virtually an original construction, inspired to be sure by his remarks but definitely going beyond them. I only hope that it will strike the reader who knows the whole development of transcendental philosophy as the only interpretive horizons in which to understand Merleau-Ponty's contribution as essentially necessary.

CONTENTS

ABBREVIATIONS

AD   *Les Aventures de la Dialectique (The Adventures of the Dialectic)*

HT   *Humanisme et Terreur (Humanism and Terror)*

PP   *La Phénoménologie de la perception (The Phenomenology of Perception)*

S   *Signes (Signs)*

SC   *La Structure du comportement (The Structure of Behavior)*

SNS   *Sens et non-sens (Sense and Nonsense)*

TM   *Les Temps Modernes* (the review edited by Sartre and Merleau-Ponty, and later by Sartre alone)

CHAPTER 1

The Transcendental Viewpoint

THE CRITIQUE OF REASON—PURE OR OTHERWISE

CRITICAL PHILOSOPHY is inevitably transcendental in its viewpoint. With the realization that some of my thoughts do not represent the grasp of things as they are in themselves, but are rather only just my thoughts, must inevitably come the further realization that all the things of my experience are phenomena—that is, that for me being is perceived-being. With this further awareness comes naturally the quest for criteria interior to experience, now understood phenomenally, by which the reality and irreality of various sorts of experience can be determined. After the *Critique of Pure Reason* had brought the first set of implications to a state of high awareness, the *Critique of Practical Reason* left little doubt about the nature of such ultimate criteria. Any criterion for truth in transcendental philosophy is inevitably practical, and the sense of what it means for a truth to work is itself developed interiorly to transcendental, phenomenal experience.

The story of this suite of developments has become too familiar to astonish. One point is surprising, however, for we have had to await the generation of phenomenologists after Husserl to realize it clearly: despite the fact that a philosophy attempts to be transcendental—attacking the pretensions of pure Reason, justly claiming, like *Ideen zur einer Phänomenologie,* to be transcendental phenomenological idealism, and fully realizing, as does Husserl's *Krisis,* that somehow the theoretical is rooted in the practical—it may nevertheless fail to be fundamental. A transcendental philosophy that bills itself as presuppositionless and critical may pile reduction upon reduction and still remain the victim of the commonsense viewpoint it has worked so hard to neutralize.

Hegel's criticism of Kant already implied that a philosophy can be genuinely critical and transcendental—in the sense of considering what appears precisely in terms of the consciousness' bringing its object into being—and still assume everyday commonsense convictions, thus making presuppositions about the nature of experience instead of radically questioning its significance. As Hegel sees it, Kant's every affirmation of the phenomenon-noumenon distinction is an uncritical giving in to the commonsense conviction that there really are things-in-themselves and that, even though we are unable to say just what they are, they make their reality felt.

Hegel, banishing the thing-in-itself, succeeds in being still more fundamental. Gone are the last traces of subject-object opposition; the matter is now authentically informed as the very sense of the dialectic is worked up out of the insufficiencies of each moment of signification, and the necessity (*Notwendigkeit*) of its forward movement receives its drive from the demonstrated need (*Not*) of each figure for another, often apparently contrary one to fulfill its sense. An index of the fundamental importance of Hegelian analysis can be found in its ability to integrate human phenomena of many levels, from basic epistemological-logical formations to the most specific artistic and literary creations, into one scheme of explanation, in which the voluntary and the intellectual, the temporal and the eternal, the natural and the cultural are intimately intertwined.

Yet Hegel himself—without whose fundamental ontology the later phenomenology would be unthinkable—did not succeed in reducing all commonsense convictions to neutrality. He left unexamined the conviction that being must make sense. For him what is became simply what is known; he always sought the logos of the phenomena in total explanation. Hegel constantly tends to dissipate the opaqueness of Being, to turn away from the resistant, the paradoxical, the impenetrable, and to affirm an ideal world, a universe of intelligible order that is a totally human production.

The proto-existentialists were able to offer in opposition to Hegel's apotheosis of reason as Being itself only their feeling that somehow things do not in fact actually make as much sense as Hegel supposed they ought to; and they expressed in dramatic terms their conviction that men are not so much Spirit in general as individual persons, not just Reason but reasoning beings; that each individual is a concrete ego, with its personal history, its lacunae, its point of view, its peculiar destiny—a partly opaque reality not to be absorbed in the whole, but resisting reflective grasp, the way things themselves appear to resist total penetration by consciousness. Thus, there is actually a whole critique of reason to be found in the works of Kierkegaard and Nietzsche; but, being unsystematic and frenetic, it was destined to remain poorly understood until phenomenology had more methodically prepared the ground.[1]

Even in the heyday of German idealism, nineteenth-century rationalism remained a force behind the rapid developments in science. The scientist proceeded, like the commonsense man, as though he were concerned with an unequivocal reality lying there objectively before him, waiting to be known exactly as it is in itself. What was not yet known could, in principle, come to be so; in any event, nothing was considered worthy of serious attention until it had been grasped clearly, unequivocally—that is, until one encountered something which revealed itself to be exactly what it is. Since the twentieth-century revolution in physics, it is difficult even in the most objective scientific sphere, to be quite that naïve. In the areas that touch man and his knowledge, above all psychology, it ought to be simply impossible.

Nevertheless, there are still psychologists today who proceed to reflect on phenomena of the human psyche as though they had to do with objects, with things-in-themselves, analyzable into data, absolutely intelligible nodules which can be recomposed into the original experience according to some perfectly intelligible plan. I am

1. Today we can afford to admit that Hegel sought to integrate an element of otherness, concreteness, individuality, passivity into his philosophy—but, of course, without compromising the transcendental viewpoint. The proto-existentialists were impressed only by his apparent idealism and hence mounted an extensive counterattack against an opponent more unequivocally idealist than the author of *The Phenomenology of the Spirit* in fact is. This is why, too, they prefer to attack the *Logic* rather than the *Phenomenology*.

purposely overstating what is more a tendency than a clearly grasped conviction, but, after all, it was Edmund Husserl's disillusion with just such psychologism that brought him to transcendental philosophy. In no other order of experience is the break with the commonsense, objectivist, thing-in-itself attitude so strongly invited as in psychological reflection, and the fact that so many psychologists still refuse to see the need to inquire into the very conditions of our having any experience and into the sense thereof should in itself astonish us into asking why the grip of the commonsense objectivist attitude is so tenacious.

In taking up a critical direction himself, Husserl emphasized the great difficulty of breaking completely with the engagements and presuppositions of common sense, including those sanctified by scientism. He seems from the start to have realized that the human reality is fundamentally a being-in-the-world, oriented toward praxis and rooted in the will to live, and there is a suggestion of existentialism in his very insistence on the need for a conscious, ever-renewed act of rupture (*epoché*). To understand how it is that we can make things present to ourselves, we must counter-will a resistance to the spontaneous (because habitual) movement which normally plunges us into the life of the product of those acts, inducing us to believe in the things themselves as we live them to the hilt. Husserl never intended to deny a scrap of the evidence of common experience, but, on the contrary, hoped to achieve an explicit hold on the nature and ultimate implications of that experience. In order to attain such a grasp, however, the pretensions of the commonsense world had themselves to be made into an object of consideration, becoming suspended in order to be scrutinized and finally grasped on their own ultimate transcendental ground.

It is fatal to the project of phenomenology either to leave unexamined the slightest particle of commonsense belief or to refuse to consider any portion of commonsense experience. Paradoxically, a failure in the first instance produces a failure in the second; a commonsense presupposition uncriticized will always block our consideration of a whole region of experience to which it holds the key. As Merleau-Ponty explains, commonsense acceptance of the results of our intentional acts is a failure to probe into the grounds, and thus into the ultimate sense, of those results.

The irony in Husserl's case is that, despite his unceasing warning against such disaster, this very philosopher who damned psychologism for its presumption that in reflecting on experience it was dealing with things in themselves, was himself the victim—until almost the end of his career—of perhaps the most fundamental presupposition of all those with which common sense builds its world of clear objects: the assumption that what is is scientifically intelligible. It was indeed against this ultimate presupposition of Hegelianism that the proto-existentialists had unleashed their harangues. Merleau-Ponty terms it "the presupposition of reason." It should be made clear that those who criticize Husserl's *Ideen* I in this regard are not complaining that it is foolish to think that what is is in some sense reasonable, but that Husserl failed to recognize this belief for what it was: a presupposition in favor of being—*présomption en faveur de l'être,* as Merleau-Ponty puts it. This rendered him insensitive to just those aspects of experience that appear to challenge such a principle. *Ideen* I is permeated with the confidence that, once the essence of the transcendental acts of intentional consciousness has been uncovered, we shall know just how our experience is composed and shall thus hold the key to Being itself, in all its clarity and absoluteness. The problem is once again that of *The Phenomenology of the Spirit:* the tendency to give little more than lip service to the noema's opposing opacity, disparities, and uncertainties, and, while paying loud tribute to the patient and painful work of Spirit, to reduce its opposing otherness to itself. By advancing the cause of absolute explanation far beyond anything the paradox of actual perceptual experience can authorize, such confidence hides from view the significant mysteries attending the coming-to-be that occurs in perception.

Merleau-Ponty never hid the debt he owed to Hegel, Husserl, and of course Kant, but he learned their lessons so well that he was prepared to deepen his critique beyond theirs, until even the presumption of reason itself was made to show its credentials. His quest was single-mindedly and unwaveringly a search for *le fondamental,* and no philosophy in the long tradition leading from Descartes through transcendental philosophy to the flowering of phenomenology can lay claim more justly to having pushed fundamental ontology to an absolute ground where not one uncriticized particle is left to common sense.

This radicalization of the basic approach (*problématique*, in Merleau-Ponty's terms) of critical philosophy beyond the achievements of either Hegel or Husserl was not simply the result of Merleau-Ponty's very great personal creativity. Certain elements in his personality and history do of course throw light on his existentialism and on his skepticism à la Montaigne concerning schemes of reason that would explain all phenomena by bringing them under a single, clear, utterly self-possessed Idea. Sartre's memorial article[2] reveals the value of such personal commentary. But the impact of events and personality traits on a philosophy, however concrete it aspires to be, can be appreciated only when one has a critical hold on the technical philosophical pressures—especially the fundamental ontological ones —in the philosophies and the psychologies that begot it, for these, as Heidegger would say, form the horizons of its historical happening (*Geschehen*).

In this regard, there can be no hesitation in saying that one philosopher more than dominates—indeed haunts—both Merleau-Ponty and Sartre: the master spirit of the French schools, Descartes, truly the ultimate father of transcendental philosophy. This is tantamount to admitting that the whole tradition was born under the sign of absolute explanation, for familiarity with the *Meditations* brings one to a realization of what it means to explain—to bring a phenomenon under a principle so absolute, so unchanging, so simple that it needs no other in order to exist. After wrestling with Descartes, one can never again be satisfied with a less exigent standard of explanation. On the other hand, the price of absolute rational possession is also clearly indicated by the Cartesian tradition: the principle tends to absorb what it is supposed to explain; the mode of the finite substance seems as nothing compared to the absolute substance itself; or, in Hegelian terms, it becomes impossible to understand ultimately the actual ontological

2. Jean-Paul Sartre, "Merleau-Ponty Vivant," *Les Temps Modernes*, 17 (1961), 304–76; trans. Benita Eisler, *Situations* (New York, Braziller, 1965), pp. 225–326.

status of the *Gestalten* through which the Spirit has passed once "The Absolute Idea" has been realized. Thus the study of Descartes and, for that matter, Hegel in post-Nietzschean times can have the effect of forcing one to realize the need to underscore everything in experience which, through its stubborn otherness, can resist absorption into the ground of explanation.

The French tradition itself has spawned its own antirationalist counterattack, prepared before Descartes by Montaigne, renewed by Pascal, and apparent even in our own day in a Gabriel Marcel; the unique, the purely personal, the authentically mysterious have not lacked convincing spokesmen. When the students of the *École Normale* in Merleau-Ponty's generation added Freud to their classical *agrégation* fare, it made it all the more difficult for them to accept the overly univocal explanations of positivistic psychologies and empiricist philosophies spawned by declining Cartesianism.

Projected against this background, the complex bearing of the other main influences on Merleau-Ponty—Husserl, Gestalt psychology, Hegel, Marx, and, of course, Heidegger—becomes much clearer.[3]

Despite our complaint that Husserl, at least until his very last period, remained influenced by the uncriticized commonsense presumptions that accept absolute explanation, we must not forget his devotion to and genius for description of subordinate moments; he remained convinced of their importance and therefore allowed them to resist absorption by the Explanatory Principle. In clarifying such moments, his phenomenological quest for essences resulted in a fierce tension that moved him toward an increasingly existential presentation of his ultimate categories; at the same time, his deep Cartesianism prevented his being attracted to the more superficial positivistic rationalism that results from a partial comprehension of Descartes.

3. (For Marx, see below, Chapter 4.) This list is not exclusive, of course. Bergson's influence is everywhere; Valéry influenced the Sartre–Merleau-Ponty circle tremendously. So did Saussure, for the theory of language (see Chapter 5). So, in many little ways, did Max Scheler. Finally, one should never forget Proust who did as much as any pure philosopher to create the climate that produced French existentialist phenomenology. We have traced the philosophical side of this development in Etienne Gilson, Thomas Langan, and Armand Maurer, *Recent Philosophy* (New York, Random House, 1966).

From Husserl, then, Merleau-Ponty learned both the meaning of radical and methodical exploration of our experience from the transcendental viewpoint and the ultimate danger of an intellectualization that renders the founding term insubstantial. The Gestalt psychologists offered a suggestion he was to develop into a possible corrective of the Husserlian form of the classical Cartesian difficulty. This was their notion that the synthesizing forms of our experience are not ideas but corporeal a prioris. These givens of the body, physiological forms which establish the general horizons of the world of our experience, prepare the possibility of intellectual knowledge but are effective prior to it and as its ground; they are themselves moments of Being.

The Gestalt psychologists did not sufficiently explore the philosophical implications of their discovery, to their own detriment. Merleau-Ponty, aided by Husserl to see the intentional nature of the Gestaltist discovery, attempted to. Inspired particularly by Kurt Goldstein's *Der Aufbau des Organismus,* Merleau-Ponty, in his first book, *The Structure of Behavior,* utilizes the Gestaltist notion of the figure-background (figure-fond) dialectic in his effort to keep his explanation of experience from crystallizing into fixed concepts. Greatly oversimplified, his interpretation is that the background is formed of the sedimented general results of all the body's previous dialogues with Being; its articulations are differentiations achieved by Being in its own mass. The figure stands at the center of the perceptive space opened by the body—an opening hollowed by Being itself, the "sides," "horizons," or "fond" of which are the whole of Being. The implications as well as the sense of this view of the central Gestaltist notion will occupy our attention throughout the present study. By way of introduction it should be sufficient to remark that for Merleau-Ponty, as he himself declared in a note written only months before his death, "the Gestalt holds the key to the problem of the spirit."

Drawing heavily on Gestaltist evidence that human comportment, while maintaining a properly organic unity, also manifests certain dialectically interrelated levels, *The Structure of Behavior*—in accord with the Husserlian conviction that before we can hope to disengage the sense of the ultimate unity of the spirit's total life, we must attend to the many essences of the different regions within incarnated existence—explores an organization supple enough to look "down"

toward the many different moments of experience and "up" toward
their ultimate unity in a conscious life which manages not to suppress
the importance of its moments and which "never transcends completely the contingency of its own giveness."[4] But even here the tight-
rope between rationalism and empiricism is hard to walk; the particular form must be criticized for its tendency to impose itself like a
thing, but, on the other hand, it must not be abandoned to the idealist
tendency of consciousness to absorb it into an undifferentiated unity.
This problem had been acute for Husserl, especially in *Krisis,* and was
even more so for his students, Heidegger, and the younger phenomenologists Sartre, Merleau-Ponty, Ricoeur, and Dufrenne. All these
thinkers are as incapable as Hegel of forgetting just how fundamental,
how unitary, the absolute principle of consciousness must be and, at
the same time, as aware as Kierkegaard and Nietzsche of the incredibly
variegated and resisting multiplicity with which the contingent founding experience is given. The tentative position toward which the last
works of Husserl were cautiously tending was already, in 1927, radically undertaken by his successor to the Freiburg chair, Martin Heidegger, in his masterwork *Being and Time (Sein und Zeit).* That work
profited from the central lesson of *The Phenomenology of the Spirit:*
only an analysis of the ultimate horizons of our experience in terms of
their historicity can descriptively unveil a structure flexible enough
to enfold all the variegated moments of that experience without reducing them to an univocal unity.

Is it then to *Being and Time* that we should turn if we want to
know the immediate source of Merleau-Ponty's philosophy? Tempting
as it is to affirm simply that Heidegger is the true guiding spirit of

4. The position Merleau-Ponty develops in *SC* owes much both to
Husserl's notion of *Fundierung* (which we shall discuss in Chapter 2) and the
compatible, although independently arrived at, physiological-psychological
conclusions of the organismic school, of which Kurt Goldstein is the most
prominent representative. For a condensed discussion of the theory of the
whole organism's seeking to fulfill its ends by substituting for damaged parts
of the brain and for a statement of a more dialectical theory of "localizations,"
along with the notion of the functions of layers in the outer cortex, see K.
Goldstein, *Language and Language Disturbances* (New York, Grave and
Stratton, 1948), pp. 45–55.

The Phenomenology of Perception, the whole truth is more complex. In-der-Welt-Sein is indeed the central focus of Merleau-Ponty's principal work, and it is Heidegger's masterpiece which provides the inspiration for both Sartre's and Merleau-Ponty's meditations on our being-in-the-world as essentially an existential act, the ground of all liberty and source of the very possibility of truth. But Merleau-Ponty's work is in no sense a mere gloss on a text of Martin Heidegger. In the first place, Sartre's *Being and Nothingness* had intervened, underscoring in a highly original way the nihilistic propensities of existentialism. *The Phenomenology of Perception* is certainly intended to combat this nihilism by arriving at an answer to Sartre's idealism, just as Heidegger's later works have been concerned to establish that the Heideggerian *Denken* overcomes (*überwindet*) the nihilism inherent in the "evening of the *abendländische Metaphysik.*" While Heidegger considered Nietzsche to be the principal incarnation of the end of metaphysics, he did once, in answer to a question of Jean Beaufret, explicitly include Sartre's humanism in this category,[5] as well he might. It is one of those ironies that transform the history of philosophy into a suite of paradoxes that Sartre, student of Heidegger and existentialist par excellence, instead of criticizing transcendental philosophy for those latent presuppositions which urge it toward idealism, rather embraced them himself in *Being and Nothingness.* His demonstration of the voluntaristic and nihilistic elements in transcendental idealism gave Merleau-Ponty some measure of the need for a profounder critique. What happened to Sartre, indicated that the Heideggerian *Grund* itself needed some firmer grounding.

Even before *Being and Nothingness* had been written, *The Structure of Behavior* had laid the groundwork for Merleau-Ponty's central contribution—the notion of an existent, who, instead of being conceived as self-transparent *pour soi* and self-creative negative will, too much outside of being for one to be able to speak of its opening on to being, is of the world as well as genuinely in it. Incarnated, living, meaningful matter, intention ineluctably involved with a re-

---

5. In *The Letter on Humanism.* On Heidegger's theory of the end of metaphysics, see my *The Meaning of Heidegger* (New York, Columbia University Press, 1959), pp. 176–214.

sisting *adversité*, the existent is a part of being turning back on itself. Goldstein had shown that the structured ground of an organism is not nothing and also that the otherness that is the living thing's milieu is not absolutely foreign to it; rather, the sense that the ground has for the organism varies according to the kind of structure the living thing brings to the dialogue. Freud suggested that consciousness wells up from and depends on depths which are not all as illumined by the self as the ideas which stand at the center of awareness. *The Structure of Behavior* fuses these suggestions into a preliminary exploration that clearly founds a fundamental ontology and concludes by describing human comportment as the opening of a world in which there is space for Being to appear.

The focus of *The Phenomenology of Perception*—an attempt to found an ontology that would overcome definitively the old oppositions of idealism-empiricism—undoubtedly results in part from Merleau-Ponty's ever-sharpening awareness of the problems of Sartre's ontology. But Merleau-Ponty's masterpiece cannot be considered fairly as a mere corrective to Sartre; nor, as we shall see, is it merely a development of a possible direction sketched out by Heidegger, a savant exploration of directions suggested by Husserl in *Krisis* and in the unpublished manuscripts, a phenomenological reexploration of Freud's ground with special efforts at clearing up any equivocations that might lead to an objectivist interpretation of the psychoanalyst's doctrine, an effort to save the living dialectic of *The Phenomenology of the Spirit* from the absolute necessity of the logic or material dialectic vivified by Gestaltist insights. In undertaking all of these tasks, it became the epicenter of an original horizon-opening philosophy situated in the mainstream of the western philosophical tradition stretching from Kant and Hegel through Husserl and Heidegger. Indeed, this philosophy may, more than Heidegger's, prove to be the fundamental ontology, the radical criticism, called for by *Being and Time*.

A clear measure of its originality may be obtained by focusing on that central concern of philosophies in the transcendental tradition, the synthesis by which the intentional agent provides the horizons in which things may appear.

A New Notion of Synthesis

In seeking to take explicit possession of Being, transcendental philosophy recognizes that it must deal with, not a reality-in-itself, but our experience. In other words, it has to do with phenomena and must recognize "that which is" to be a result of a positing act of experience on our part. Kant, because he recognized time as the central form of our existence, termed this positing an act of synthesis. In a time-spanning, sense-creating act, the existent synthesizes present perceptual data, past experiences, and anticipatory-interpretative schemes into that persisting unity we call a thing. Likewise, the many things are synthesized into propositions, and the many propositions into a world of signification.

Transcendental philosophy must perforce be centrally concerned with the adequate description of the relationship between the synthesizing act and that which is synthesized. (Not, it is essential to note, "between subject and object," for one of the principal signs that transcendental philosophy has advanced beyond earlier rationalist epistemologies lies in its realization that such a distinction is disastrously misleading.) It is an act of the cognitive subject which makes possible all objectivity, but, on the other hand, no matter how subjective (i.e., personal, fanciful, etc.) such an act might be, it depends in some way on the data it organizes. Since it must result in an organization of those data, every intentional act essentially escapes itself, transcends toward that which it produces, rejoining other acts and their products (other things) and taking up their sense in order to have sense itself. In short, transcendental philosophy discovers from the start that some of the objectivity of the commonsense thing is present in every intentional act's product and, at the same time, that the teleological, the creative, the subjective enters in the cognition of even the most objective object. Thus the fundamental human act is neither pure creativity nor mere passive receptivity, neither simply voluntary nor ever completely free of subjectivity. It is both individual and yet universally relevant, resulting in the possession of a truth valid for other men, perhaps for all men, but always held from a point of view. Such an act is a phenomenon of the moment which still can contain a sense for all time.

Kant discovered that our *Erfahrung* is an affair neither of sense nor of intellect alone, but of both together; that the form of the process by which passively received data is actively formed into a whole through the mediation of *Einbildungskraft,* the power of synthesizing-imagining, is space-time, and he even suggests that what we are and what we aspire to somehow enter into the sense of the intentional whole. But Merlau-Ponty complains that Kant, wishing to explain "how in general a world is possible," sought for the explanation in "a source of signification (*sens*)" prior to the world, to which, through reflection, the philosopher could return and which he could thus come consciously to possess (*PP,* p. 254; *VI,* p. 74 n.). Time tends to remain in Kant's philosophy a formal organizing principle, one which does not itself affect intimately the sense of the world.

Hegel's deformalization of time showed the coming-to-be of the sense of the world as a reciprocal relationship, in which the sensegiver discovers himself progressively in and through the sense with which he has already endowed the world. For the interrogation of the world is Being's interrogation of itself, Being's own becoming.

But the dialectical approach does not automatically eradicate the temptation to posit a kind of en soi, an unequivocal once-and-for-all reality. Renouncing its true vocation as the continual self-interrogation and revelation of Being, the dialectic may seek to formulate itself definitively and finally; the negativity that is at work in the dialectic process is then absolutized, becoming self-negation; concomitantly, Being falls back into pure positivity, becoming just what it is, *être en soi.* The absolutized negativity is seen as denying itself in order that the world might be, thus allowing the absolute to view itself. The dialectic then becomes "a pure identity of opposites, ambivalence" (*VI,* p. 127) in becoming *chose dite,* a thesis, it ceases to practice that perpetual following of Being's autoconstitution which alone brings out the sense of a truly temporal world (*VI,* p. 128).

Hegel's absolute tends to impose such a structure rather than to espouse an actual movement of Being itself; it tends to become ego, declaring by fiat what it wants the sense of things to be, rather than perceiver, codiscovering with Being its own hidden depths. The explanatory principle thus absorbs what it is supposed to explain, including the elements of passivity, individual creativity, opacity, and obscurity, instead of showing their intelligible, if not merely rational sense. It was, of course, precisely those elements that Kierkegaard and Nietzsche were to flaunt in their existential revolution.

But the danger of absorbing, as Descartes did, the inferior, the dependent elements of the appearing world into the ultimate spiritual principle of the Ego which provides their final explanation is not finally exorcised by the existentialist approach either. What Descartes did with the Divine Substance, Kant with the Transcendental Unity of Apperception, Fichte with *Ich-Ich,* Hegel with *Geist,* and Husserl with the Transcendental Ego, the existential phenomenologist is tempted to do with his ultimate principle, the freedom of the existent. While the earlier transcendental philosophers fell easily into absolute idealism, the existentialist is faced with the danger of voluntaristic subjectivism in which the finite human will becomes the absolute thing, the bestower of all sense. Heidegger resists the temptation heroically by insisting on the distinction between *das Sein* (Being) and *die Seienden* (the beings); whether he is successful or not is a question we shall seek to answer at the end of this study. The Sartre of *L'Etre et le Néant,* on the other hand, seems to throw himself gleefully into the trap, and Merleau-Ponty's contribution is an original formula for avoiding the pitfalls his work reveals. Whether we can afford the price at which this success is purchased is the ultimate critical question of the present study.

At the center of Merleau-Ponty's contribution lies the view that the world-opening horizons through which Being reveals itself are founded, not by a principle of absolute negativity (whether conceived as infinite transcendental Ego or as finite sense-giving will), but rather as the result of a formation within Being achieved by Being itself. In living the world, we perceive the coming-to-be of a sense within Being. Our bodies are part of the world, are aspects of Being itself through which a consciousness is made possible. And while the reflective space which is thus opened within Being may tend to consider itself apart, as though this point of consciousness were somehow source of all that is, or at least absolute creator of its sense; and although it hides the "brute Being" under accumulated layers of the sedimented results of its organizing dialogues with *l'être sauvage,* we must, and can, learn to seek out the fundamental, the *Urpräsentierbar* (*VI*, p. 272[6]), the nature that still shows through gaps in the culture that has been woven from parts of it.

The Phenomenology of Perception, in setting out in search of the fundamental coming-to-be of Being, explores radically the peculiar mode of our corporeal Being-in-the-world. As such, it constitutes, in Merleau-Ponty's own words, "a new transcendental aesthetic" (*PP,* p. 254). Here, no vestige of form imposing itself on matter remains, but, instead, the dialectical reciprocity of the founding and founded acts at every level of consciousness is established as a phenomenon attesting to the oneness of Being (see Chapter 2, Aesthetica). The inherent finitude of the perceptual synthesis is underlined, with great emphasis on the figure's essential dependence for its very sense upon a background (fond) of structuring possibilities, the horizons of which always escape the ego's explicit comprehension because they are the positive totality of Being itself. It follows that the pretensions of rational judgments to pronounce eternally on the way things are in themselves must lack absolute validity, and that their value is essentially practical (see Chapter 3, Analytica-Dialectica). Against these absolutistic pretensions and in the light of the *Phenomenology's* ontological discovery that *esse est percipi,* and is thus an act, the liberty of the human existent can then be revealed as the concrete principle of initiative which, to realize itself authentically, must in espousing its situation respect Being (see Chapter 4, Practica, The Problem of Finite Freedom). The overriding importance of the concrete situation as real ground for positing a truth having been established, the political essays, *Humanism and Terror* and *The Adventures of the Dialectic,* can be studied as the sort of analyses of concrete political situations which alone can provide the full measure of what it means to make the truth come to be (*la vérité est à faire*) (see Chapter 4, The Human Nature of the World's Demands). Armed with this concrete vision of an existential truth at work, we shall turn finally to the last essays (*Signs*), a kind of counterpart of the *Critique of Judgment,* where it becomes strikingly clear why this transcendental philosophy begins as transcendental aesthetic but ends in aestheticism

6. "L'Etre d'indivision . . . le sensible creusé dans l'être sans restriction."

(see Chapter 5, Poetica: A New Montaigne). We shall see that it is indeed true that "L'existentialisme est un humanisme," and that humanism—at least in this sense—finds it difficult to avoid altogether a certain scepticism.

This volume is not intended to be an introduction to all the rich variety of themes interwoven in the philosophy of Merleau-Ponty nor is it an attempt to trace the development of his grasp on the ontological implications of a position still in embryo in the first works. Rather, it is an inquiry pointed directly at the central notions of Merleau-Ponty's ontology. Insights into particular problems will be presented in the light of the mature position and with a view to understanding it. Our final aim is to see what light the contributions and the difficulties of this ontology can cast on the whole tradition of transcendental philosophy from Kant through Hegel and Husserl.

CHAPTER 2

Incarnated Intentionality: The New Transcendental Aesthetic

THE PROBLEM OF TRUTH

EVEN BEFORE THE CARTESIAN REVOLUTION, classical realism, comfortably ensconced in the certitudes of common sense, had already encountered a truth problem: Given the existence of real things-in-themselves, how can these things take up their abode in the spirit, and, correlatively (since every question about truth is always also implicitly a question about error), if what I know are really objective things as they are in themselves, how can I ever be in error about them? Transcendental philosophy has turned the question around: Given that what we know are our representations (phenomena), how can we believe commonsensically that what we know are real things-in-themselves, and why is it that many men can adhere to the same convictions about certain things—in a word, how can there be any enduring, intersubjective, objective truth? The problem of error becomes similarly reversed: How can we possibly speak of deviation from the norm of objective reality, since our problem is to know how, from inside an individual personal experience, we can ever come to be sure there are things-in-themselves "out there" at all; and how the existence of things-in-themselves, which is revealed only through interior experience, can manifest itself independent of that experience. Instead of merely acknowledging the fact that he pretends to possess a truth—a reality somehow independent of himself—the transcendental philosopher seeks to take philosophical possession of the truth by inquiring into its ground and the limits of its pretensions.

St. Thomas wrote often of intentionality; to him *intendere* signifies the mind's going out to grasp the really existing thing as it actually is, the act by which the objective thing existing in itself is endowed with an *esse intentionale* so as to exist in a spirit. But offhandedly understanding Husserl's *Intentionalität* in that sense would be like a Ptolemaic interpretation of Galileo, for the transcendental philosopher sees intentionality as the synthetic act by which the phenomenon is made to be. The two viewpoints thus pose the problem of transcendence in opposite ways: for realism, objective being existing en soi transcends all the categories of thought; it is that which founds their very possibility. For phenomenology, the transcendental structures of being are themselves due to the cognitive synthesizing, which raises the problem of discovering how the cognitive act can pose for itself objects which reveal themselves as in some way transcending the very act which brings them to be.

This truth problem of transcendental philosophy becomes Merleau-Ponty's main concern, around which revolves his entire philosophy, for it is, in his eyes, the central task of philosophy today.[1] The success with which a philosopher explores this paradox holds the key to the validity of his convictions about fundamental reality—the basic, intentional relation between synthesizing and synthesized, in a word, perception. But the very formula in which Merleau-Ponty casts the truth problem, "How can there be *de l'être en soi pour nous?*" is itself already pointing the way beyond transcendental philosophy, out of the impasse to which a classical idealist-empiricist alternative led. It is an attempt to return to the fundamental in order to extricate philosophy from the mechanism-voluntarism opposition of the classic subject-object dichotomy. It is meant to avoid the root error committed by both idealism and empiricism: that of assuming this dichotomy unreflectingly from commonsense experience, rather than exploring

---

1. Merleau-Ponty explicitly states this to be the essential task. "If the return to the *Lebenswelt,*" he writes in *Signs*, ". . . is considered absolutely necessary, then philosophy must reflect on the mode of the presence of the object to the subject, the conception of the object and the conception of the subject as they appear to phenomenological revelation, instead of substituting the rapport of the object to the subject such as it is conceived in an idealist philosophy of total reflexion." *S,* p. 116.

the reality en soi of things. On the one hand, empiricism falls into the error of "choseism," dealing with things as though they were simply there, unequivocal, independent of the concrete subject and of the individual moment of experience, which are then looked upon as merely relative to the thing; at the opposite pole, idealism shifts the ground of the absolute reality en soi to the subject and then presumes the subject to be the legislator of an unequivocal truth that somehow is one for all knowers (PP, p. 278), the "somehow" being dealt with by imagining a kind of mind in general that is no one and nowhere. The contingency of the individual knower's encounter—the particularity of his point of view—with the reality known only partially is thereby rendered incomprehensible. So too is the fact that the concrete ego is partly opaque even to himself, for he can know himself only in his partial acts and can come to know himself better only as he proceeds through life. Empiricism renders the phenomenon of our finite freedom incomprehensible by threatening to absorb the subject in a datum existing so much in itself that the knower has only to register and combine the unequivocal givens; everything is as determined as it is clear. On the other hand, the intellectualism common to the classical idealists and to the phenomenologists destroys that freedom by making the subject so unequivocally in itself that its sense-giving acts seem incapable of error or even partialness; in such a subject there is literally no room for opinion, becoming, history, or concreteness.

The notion of reality en soi pour nous avoids these pitfalls because by demanding as prerequisite to any philosophy the analysis of that moment where subject and object are founded, before the dichotomy has yet been made—namely, the moment of originative perception—it poses the proper problem: how, within an experience really personal (because mine) can there arise the perception of an object, proposed to me and presenting itself existing in a world shared by others? The Phenomenology of Perception thus proposes the difficult task of a radical reflection, capable of probing below later, founded acts of cognition to reveal the primordial perceptual encounter that must take place before the subject-object distinction can be crystallized. In Merleau-Ponty's words, it is an attempt to "bring consciousness face to face with its unreflective life in things, and to wake it to awareness of its own history" (*PP,* p. 40). Or, in the still deeper sense of the last essays, it is the search for *l'être sauvage,* for the first coming-to-be of Being.

FIGURE, FIELD, AND WORLD

The Gestalt psychologists have shown that what we encounter in our primordial perceptual experience is neither the univocal, isolatable atoms of sensation postulated by empirical psychology nor the unequivocal objects presumed by common sense. Rather, the world presents itself at each instance as a meaningful totality in which the moments possess their sense as they function in the whole spectacle to which they contribute. Each partial view proves itself under examination part of a larger dynamic whole—the intentional totality of human experience, past and future, that is not simply our world, but the world. The perceptual object, declares the *Phenomenology* in a formula that cuts neatly across the old divisions, occurs within a perceptual field which itself is englobed by a background of world (*un certain champ perceptif sur fond de monde,* p. 279).

A simple example may help situate the thrust of this pivotal conception. Within a total perceptual spectacle I do not normally experience individual colors, shapes, or lines; a certain brightly lit yellow splotch get its first sense only from the whole configuration of the tableau it helps to compose. What I directly live is the wheat shock in the total landscape—the consideration in and for itself of the brightly lit yellow would be an unusual articulation resulting from a special way of attending to that which is spontaneously lived as a certain kind of *paysage.* Reciprocally, the whole configuration provided in this particular field structured by my attentive act in this particular way would not be the same without that particular perceptual moment—the yellow wheat shock is but one of the elements which give it the sense of an autumn landscape. The relationship between the constituted whole and the moment is reciprocal: the moment owes its sense to the whole and, the sense given by the whole is motivated by what the moments offer.

This relation is perhaps made even clearer by a comparison with language. A sentence is made up of words, but the words receive

their precise sense from the sentence, and both—the sentence as a
whole and the individual words—are part of a totality that transcends
them, a background overlapping both field and figure: The sentence
is part of a discourse, and the discourse part of a life lived in a social
historical world; besides each word is connected through the depths
("fond" has this sense, too) of its meaning to a whole history of
earlier contexts.

This simple example (supported in the *Phenomenology* by analyses
of many experiments dealing especially with perception of individual
colors and general illumination, in connection with the subject's
anticipations and his previous linguistic capacity) obviously contains
the kernel of a solution to the familiar subject-object-freedom opposition. The sensation does not confront me as an unequivocal otherness, an absolute foreigner, but as a moment of *my* experience; therefore, my attentive attitude, the nature of my interest in the spectacle
and the approach I take to it, necessarily influence the total sense of
what appears. Reciprocally, since not a single scrap of external data
ever reaches me except as an element within a prereflexive synthesis
already grounded in my first stance, the perceptual experience is
clearly mine; but, at the same time, perceptual moments are not my
voluntary production and the horizons of the spectacle lead off into
a totality of world which I—the reflective, voluntary conscious ego—
can in no way encompass and only very indirectly and partially control. While I am able to orient myself in the spectacle and even by
my initiative to decenter and recenter it, I am in no way conscious of
producing its contents, but I experience them as a series of givens;
indeed, my every act in regard to what I see is solicited by the very
spectacle whose presentation my perception nevertheless influences.
The landscape strikes me as in no sense my private possession, for my
experience is of a reality which Paul, who is standing beside me, can
apparently also possess—of a world which, for that matter, many subjects can experience simultaneously, although each only from his own
point of view. Paradoxically, in my own experience I discover a world
which possesses me more than I possess it.

A description of the intentional synthesis which conceived it as
corporeally grounded would discover a world-founding principle not
foreign to me (as it is part of the living texture of *my* body, the corps

propre) but, at the same time, not reducible to the cogito as individual center of initiative (as was the idealists' transcendental Ego), capable of enjoying an obviously public as well as a personal aspect (un corps, a body). The fundamental perceptual insertion into the world through the body, while grounding the objectivizations of fully developed reason, has its own fundamental mode—one very different from the clear and distinct ideas to which objectivizing reason aspires —and descriptions of perception in a field should clarify that mode.

The difficulties inherent in radical reflection on one's own experience account for the complex, at first rather disheartening, structure of *The Phenomenology of Perception*. Some problems arise from the very nature of intentional analysis, but the major difficulty is rooted in the habitual demands of common sense. In *Ideen* I, Husserl, in pointing out that our intentions are never without an object—I always perceive *something*, think of *something*, feel about *something*, etc.—proceeds to show that the object (noema) of the intentional act (noesis), being a correlative of that act, depends on it for its form: The same matter (*hule*)—an apple tree, for instance—is different as to noematic mode when seen, conceived, remembered, willed, etc.; but, conversely, the noesis is founded in the noema: the perception of an apple tree, for example, is not the same noetic act as the perception of a painting. Now what holds true for particular intentional acts interior to different regions of experience holds true as well for the description of the fundamental being-in-the-world with which the phenomenologist is ultimately concerned: the consideration of the noetic principle of the fundamental synthesis ("my body" as world-founding) must always go hand in hand with that of its noematic correlate (the world); indeed, the reciprocity of the two must be maintained in our descriptions as perfectly as the matter-form interpenetration in a good Aristotelian explanation.

Because of the very nature of commonsense experience, however, the system *corps propre-monde* has not come to the fore in the history of philosophy as the mediating principle between the ultimate poles of subject and object. We have yet to "learn to *feel* our bodies"[2] providing the very ground of our experience. The practical orientation of

2. The deliberately anti-Hegelian raising of *Gefühl* to a place of honor in philosophy is a hallmark of the end-period's radical critique of reason.

commonsense experience toward clear consciousness tends to polarize our attention, noetically, toward the most willful active principle—the subjective Ego as doer, grasped as intellect and will—and, noematically, toward the most structured object—the finished product of our praxis-centered daily concerns, the intellectually fixed, objectivized thing. While both the voluntary ego and objective thing implicitly depend on the actual body's living in the world and making an experience possible in the first place, the bodily synthesis nevertheless goes about its task so silently, so fundamentally, that its transcendental contribution is no more noticed than the light which illumines and thus makes possible every visible spectacle. Only unusual experiences revealing a fissure in the otherwise unrelieved atmosphere of already constructed world—the hallucination, the illusion, anything which causes the smooth unfolding of the world suddenly not to be taken so much for granted—can provide the epoché needed to suspend the practical experience's attention-absorbing hold on us.[3]

Even after we have recognized its existence, we still face a major problem in describing this world-founding action of the corps propre. Because of the noesis' absorption in the noema—or, to reverse the reciprocal relation, because the world must itself found that possibility of body which noetically animates it—because "le corps propre is in the world like the heart in the organism, animating it and nourishing it interiorally, forming with it a system (PP, p. 235), any description of it that maintains the desired reciprocity between the two principles must avoid suggesting that the intentional synthesis acts centrifugally and forces a sense on indifferent matter. The wonder of intentionality's noesis-noema relationship lies precisely in the fact that this Sinngebung is centrifugal and centripetal at the same time. This will explain what might otherwise seem an inconsistency in Merleau-Ponty's work. This sentence, for example, found in Signs—"the signification animates the word as the world animates my body" (S, p. 112)—might seem to contradict directly The Phenomenology of Perception's "the body animates the world." The key to the apparent paradox lies in

3. Epoché is Husserl's term for the act of suspending the normal, habitual movement of common sense out into the world of its daily practical concerns, in order to make it possible to reflect on the very possibility of there being such a world for us in the first place.

the reciprocity of the elements in intentionality. In the first quotation "my body" refers to the principle of incarnation as ground of my existence in the world as *this individual,* and my individual existence is dependent on the world's already having a general sense. In the second quotation the anonymous body is referred to as existential source of the world's general horizons. The body does indeed give the world a sense—but not arbitrarily just any sense, rather a sense "adherent in certain contents" (*PP,* p. 172), which sense is, so to speak, made for the very things which appear in its field. But to assume the moments in experience must therefore possess certain qualities en soi would be to destroy at once the much-needed equilibrium. The active moments in perception—the act of attention, the higher acts of ego—rework, take up again a sense (*reprendre,* as we shall see, is the key term) that is already latent in the givens because the body originally animates the spectacle in its own way; this is the significance of the extremely important declaration, "My body is the common texture of all the objects" (*PP,* p. 272).[4] The affirmation of the impossibility of severing the here-and-now givens from their sense, contributed by the whole texture of the body,[5] is the sole hope, as Merleau-Ponty sees it, of escaping the subject-object dilemma. It elaborates a notion of Sinngebung that is at once conscious of the revelations of the transcendental viewpoint (hence centrifugal) and capable of accommodating the facts of passivity, newness, otherness (hence centripetal). Moreover, such a Sinngebung, providing the world and at the same time provided by the world, is no Heideggerian *nichtiges Nichts,* no Kantian empty general form (for how can a form be without determination, i.e. without matter?), but a concrete-general principle with its own opacity, an ego that is genuinely incarnated in time and space, a definite comportment.

4. "My body" in most contexts means le corps propre as ground of all that is general, "anonymous," prepersonal in the world; it is usually clear from the context when it means, on the contrary, the body as a thing objectivized reflectively by intellectual acts. We have usually conserved untranslated the term le corps propre both to avoid this possible confusion and because of the untranslatable double-play of the term "propre," which means that it is the body proper, and the body *mine,* as my "property."

5. "The perception is that *act* which creates at one and the same instant the constellation of givens and the sense which binds them." *PP,* p. 46.

The intellectualist notion of the subject may appear to have solved with elegance and with a clarity that is lacking in the corps propre solution both the problem of a reality-in-itself—conceived as ideas, objects of thought—and that of a reality-for-us—the "us" being conceived as a general transparent cogito, no more mine than yours. But the general cogito of the idealist proposal is eliminated the moment one realizes that each subject is really an individual, and the post-Freudian cannot forget that. I experience myself as opening into the world from a particular point of view; my grasp of any phenomenon is always fleeting and partial; I do not even possess myself totally but, on the contrary, will always remain a mystery to myself. The motivations that surge up in me escape the accounting of my reflection, for I am opaque just as the things in the world are opaque. I come to know myself progressively, little by little, and I can be wrong about myself, just as I can be wrong when I force the anticipations of my experience of things. Correlatively, the world I really experience bears little resemblance to the world of explicitly thought objects imagined by the idealists; nothing in my perceptual field is clear and distinct, understandably connected to everything else, nor do I explicitly will the primordial unity threading through it. "At each moment my perceptive field is filled with flickering reflections (reflets), fissures, fleeting tactile impressions which I am in no position to link with precision to the perceived context and which nevertheless I posit unhesitatingly in the world without ever confusing them with my reveries. . . . The real does not await our judgment to annex the most surprising phenomena nor to reject our most plausible imaginings" (PP, pp. iv–v).

It is this world of living experience perceived by a truly concrete "I" that Merleau-Ponty proposes to describe with the aid of the corps propre notion. The systematic effort to carry out such a phenomenology is new and challenging because of the intrinsic difficulty of using reflective tools (the only means of philosophic expression we possess) to describe what is prereflexive—using the instrument of the intellect to fix what is not intellectual because it is essentially dynamic, using the explicit abstract tools of expression to direct oneself to the immediately lived level of experience. "We must learn to feel our bodies."

Because of this paradox, the principal concepts Merleau-Ponty utilizes to direct our attention to facets of the primordial experience of intentionality will not be intellectually satisfying. Such terms as "field," "world," "ambiguity," "prehistoric," "openness," "movement," "anonymity," "existence," "motivation," "*sens,*" and "transcendence" cannot be clear and distinct and certainly are not calculated to please that within us which invites us to become idealists, whether of the early Husserlian kind or the more empiricist sort.[6] But Merleau-Ponty is convinced that a phenomenology must be prepared to grow forever; if the connotations of its key terms open for us ever wider circles of experience, even though we can never quite possess it all, if they can be *motif et matière* for thought, it has fulfilled its goal—the only possible goal of a true philosophy of experience.

THE CHARACTERISTICS OF
INCARNATED INTENTIONALITY

The Fond of the Living Perceptual Encounter

ANONYMITY The corps propre theory of perception is intended to illumine the paradox of man's active-passive participation in the coming-to-be of truth. The first problem in developing such a conception is to allow the all-pervasive transcendental mode characteristic of incarnated perception to become apparent. As a kind of epoché for this purpose, the *Phenomenology* turns to those exceptional psychological experiences in which the habits of our practically oriented and smoothly adapted everyday existence fall away for an instant.[7] At such moments we are permitted to appreciate the normal world-founding

6. Merleau-Ponty puts this even more strongly than we have here, speaking of the fundamental conception of an incarnated cogito, the ambiguous, as a contradiction, and stating flatly that ultimately his philosophy is not *pensable* (PP, pp. 418–19). I prefer to avoid confronting the reader just at the beginning with such a bald statement. We shall understand it better when we come, in due course, to discuss the transcendence of intentionality (cf. Chapter 2, para. 5, below). For now let it be noted that for this philosophy to be *impensable* is not for it *de ne rien vouloir dire.*

7. Instead of invoking the result of the exceptional situation, such as *Angst,* Merleau-Ponty lays out the clinical data which itself is enough actually to produce a kind of *Angst* in the way it dissolves the familiar.

acts through their very absence. Plunged to the point of juncture where body and world are in dialogue, we can see that each is adjusting to the other under the impulsion of the situation's evolution.

Paradoxically, such a dialogue is fully human and even individual in nature without being personal or voluntary. This is what Merleau-Ponty means when he describes the act of perception as anonymous: by providing "the texture of the things in the world," my body does indeed act, but as general principle of a common intersubjective human world. Indeed, my body is actually part of the very world whose texture it itself provides. Such a paradox can only be understood intentionally, in terms of the dialectic of noesis-and-noema. It is this fundamental reality which we must now try to glimpse.

Here is an example of such an exceptional experience, recounted by the psychologist Wertheimer in *Experimentelle Studien über das Sehen von Bewegung*. A subject was placed in a room so arranged that it could be seen only in a mirror inclined 45° from the vertical. The room at first appeared to the subject as oblique (a man seen—in the mirror—walking in the room seemed to walk on a slant; a piece of cardboard allowed to fall along the doorjamb seemed to fall in an oblique direction), but after a few minutes, the room and its contents suddenly appeared vertical, normal.

It might be suggested that the subject succeeded in reasoning himself into a new orientation. The phenomenal field is always somewhat accessible to thought, and Merleau-Ponty will never deny that explicit reasoning can be used to close abnormal gaps in behavior. But this leads to the question of why the subject should carry out any such reorientation at all. It was not necessary to his reasoning powers, for he could understand and explain any element or event in the room without explicitly thinking about his own relationship to the entire environment. Any satisfactory explanation of Wertheimer's experiment should then throw light on the general phenomenon of man's continual orientation and thus on the nature of space and its relationship to experience in general.

Here is Merleau-Ponty's interpretation: When the subject first comes before the mirror, he has nothing to do with the objects that appear there and therefore cannot be said to inhabit that space; he does not share the same room with the man he sees walking there. After a few minutes—provided he does not cast a glance outside of the field of the mirror, thus reestablishing his anchors in the normally oriented space—the reflected room evokes a subject capable of actively living within it. The resultant virtual body displaces the real body to such an extent that the subject no longer feels himself in the usual world he effectively inhabits; instead, he "lives" the legs and arms he would need to walk and act in the reflected room. Concisely, he inhabits the spectacle.

This notion is one of Merleau-Ponty's ways of conveying the reciprocity that characterizes authentic intentionality. In the fundamental existential moment, the living body and the lived world are inseparable: my body inhabits the spectacle as the soul inhabits the body.

As the soul of the spectacle, I begin as anonymous form of this matter which I shall only later reassume (*reprendre*), personalizing it in reflection and explicit self-consciousness by means of a process not unlike the Freudian progression from the subconscious to the conscious. Since my body is no mere thing, there is nothing mechanical about its adaptation to the spectacle. Its anonymity is precisely that nonpersonal humanity which is living, intentional, but not yet reflexive. Note that even though neither mechanical determination nor explicit awareness apply here, the categories of "sense" and "non-sense" (which will be explored shortly) do.

My body is important for the orientation of the spectacle, then, not simply as this particular thing in objective space with this determined relation of parts and this given attitude, but as system of possible actions, a virtual body whose phenomenal place (lieu) is defined by its task and situation. At the moment when Wertheimer's subject began "living" the reflected space vertically, what might be called his spatial level (*le niveau spatial*), the particular spatial grasp that the body has on the world, did, in effect, teeter over.

Such a *prise* normally appears at the point of junction between one's motor intentions and one's perceptive field. It occurs at the moment when one's effective body comes to coincide with the virtual body demanded by the spectacle while, at the same time, the effective spectacle coincides with the milieu projected by one's body. Such a grasp is thus a kind of pact established between, on the one hand, my body as power of certain gestures favoring certain planes of action[8] and, on the other hand, the perceived spectacle as both invitation to these gestures and theater of those actions. This pact makes it possible for me to enjoy the space, just as reciprocally it permits the things to have a direct power on my body (PP, pp. 288–89).

The very central notion of a pact is intended to bring out another aspect of the communion between the noetic act and its noematic content—the teleological one. To understand this, let us consider Wertheimer's experiment a bit further. It deals with spatial orientation in Merleau-Ponty's interpretation; this space is taken in its most transcendental sense, as *champ d'action* (the field in which action can take place), the founding of an intentional relation the members of which relate to each other and find their reciprocal sense precisely because they are able to assert their distinctness from one another. Such "taking one's distance" is the very foundation of *Ek-sistenz*. The agent's movement, his gesture, must be understood as the corporeal pole of the fundamental act of relating oneself to.

I would like to stop here an instant on the notion of "geste," the gesture which both creates and is made possible by the existentially opened space. The term suggests of course the bridging of a distance and thus (in the Bergsonian tradition) the unifying-separation in time that managing a space implies. It also invokes the anonymous ground of perception: A geste is a movement, spontaneously welling up from the corporeal spiritual depths of the individual, immediately incarnating an intention in matter, directly comprehensible by all. Physical, it is also spiritual; personal, it is also ancestrally human and general. But it is also more than a movement; often involuntary, it is a motivated movement, rather than either a willed or mechanical one. It cannot be described either as unconscious or as explicitly thought; though its sense also is not fully explicit, it is also incontestably a sense-giving process which calls data to gravitate into a meaningful constellation within the phenomenal field, excluding from this field other things which, although perhaps objectively within range of my

8. The merit of the term *gestes* is that it suggests a motricity that might serve equally well to express an intention, as to carry one out by grasping or showing something.

senses, are kept out because they have no meaning there. When I take advantage, for instance, of the "science" of my apartment that is hidden in my body—navigating, perhaps even in the dark, from my study to the kitchen without having to think about where I am going—it is clear that my goal, my perception of my present position, and my science are silently combining and adjusting at every moment to form the sense of the unifying gesture I am accomplishing. Last, but not least, "geste" in French inevitably calls to mind the phrase *beau geste,* an act which is its own reward, an act having its own aesthetic end to be kept alive forever in the *chansons de gestes* of the human community for all men of the future to take up again and imitate. In the gesture of *The Phenomenology of Perception* we thus already have the germs of the *Signs* of 1962.

Here, then, is a process which occurs in me—or, more exactly, in my body—but which in every respect transcends me in the sense of this moment of conscious awareness. It depends on a past (the science accumulated in my habits) which, according to the given modalities of the body, deploys itself in view of a goal which, though I may have chosen it, nevertheless finds its sense in rearranging all the givens my sensations are continuing to offer. Hence the meaningful, oriented space which the body opens, in which the contributions of body and world are effectively indistinguishable, is a space onto which open all human existences, through their own corporeally founded pacts with the world: it is the existential space in which all human meanings take place (*avoir lieu*).[9] The pact notion thus suppresses the old chicken-or-egg questions about determination by revealing how the very sense of the human spectacle arises in part in the science of experience already accumulated in the body, as the elements of the world are synthesized by the living corps propre, itself a product of living syntheses.

But even this notion suggests that all considerations of teleology have not fully lost their sense, for we can still ask, To what end is such a pact made?

In certain contexts intended to emphasize the fact that our perception reveals a reality existing in some sense en soi, the teleology seems,

9. Cf. below, Generality.

at first glance, almost objectivist. If the perceptive activity is for the sake of the perceived reality, then, even though the perceiver is indeed a doer and the spectacle is not indifferent to his activity, the demands of what is to be seen do motivate the appropriate activity. To take just one example, here is a classical experiment reported by Werner in *Untersuchungen über Empfindung und Empfinden*. A subject was placed in a darkened room, where he first heard the name of a color shouted and was then inundated with light of the announced color. When, after several normal experiences of this sort, "red" was announced but was in fact followed by a flood of blue light, the results were as follows: "If a subject tries to experience a determined color, for example blue, while seeking to take up the bodily attitude which agrees with red, there results an interior struggle, a sort of spasm, which ceases as soon as the corporeal attitude which agrees with blue is adopted" (*PP*, p. 248). The subject must find an attitude that will give the color the means of determining itself, and Merleau-Ponty's formula expresses the reciprocity of the relationship which renders the determined sensation possible: "The sensible returns to me what I have lent it, but it is from the sensible that I got it in the first place." The resultant relationship, he declares, is a veritable communion: I "lend an ear" to the sound which then engulfs my ear, takes it over; "I deliver up a part of my body or perhaps even my whole body to that manner of vibrating and of filling space" which is this particular sound. Now, though this description may at first appear to support a teleology oriented toward the demands of a preexisting object—in this case, the particular sound—it must be clearly understood that the sensation is a bipolar, indeed an intentional, act. I find in the sensible the proposition of a certain new rhythm of existence —abduction or adduction—and in answer to it (*lui donnant suite*), I insinuate myself into the form of existence which is thus suggested to me; thereby, I relate myself to the non-I, whether in order to open myself to it or to close myself off from it, and thus give both it and me reality and sense, forming a common pact.

The sense of this reciprocity can be clarified by another example, also drawn from a text intent on making us feel both the transcendence of the perceptual experience and its lived quality as an experience truly belonging to the corps propre. When I abandon myself to the contemplation of the infinite blue expanse of the sky, I do not deploy ahead of the experience an idea which can unlock its secret; rather, as I abandon myself to the sky, my consciousness is taken over by unlimited blue, and the sky itself begins to exist for me. Its existence is in no way that of an intellectual object—the astronomer's idea of sky, for instance, with each part clearly and distinctly separated from the others—but a living sensible whole, a "milieu of a certain vital vibration which my body adopts." Since the vibration referred to is the perceived reality itself, we might best say of the perceived sky, *il se pense en moi*—it thinks itself in me.

Without abandoning the feeling of the perceiver's action being elicited by a given, this last description underscores more strongly the realization that the sky perceived is nevertheless the act of the perceiver's body and cannot exist without it. Not only is the noema not indifferent to the mode of the noesis, but the noetic activity, it appears here, is in some sense one with the fundamental end of the pact. This allots the question of teleology its proper degree of complication!

Fortunately, *The Phenomenology of Perception* explicitly indicates that the *telos* must be recognized to be grounded in the *eidos*. Generalizing from the example of the experiment with colors, Merleau-Ponty declares that my body "gets into gear" with the world "when my perception offers me as varied and as clearly articulated a spectacle as possible and when my motor intentions in deploying themselves receive from the world the responses they were expecting. This maximum of sharpness (*netteté*) in the perception and in action defines a perceptive ground (*sol*), a fond for my life, a general milieu for the coexistence of my body and the world" (*PP*, pp. 289–90). Thus, the telos of the perception is to open the best possible milieu, that milieu which achieves "as varied and as clearly articulated a spectacle as possible." What determines that possibility is the nature of my motor intentions, as *The Structure of Behavior* makes clear in its abundantly documented contrast of the possibilities of human comportment with the more restricted possibilities of the higher animals. The best possible equilibrium worked out between me as specific ego and my incarnated situation provides the ground and the background (they are the same), the horizons within which I play out my life, a general milieu the dialectical terms of which are "my body" and "the world" as they coexist there. The fundamental ontological significance of the body-world pact begins to become manifest here, for the anonymity of the body's world-founding activity grounds the general structures of the world as the horizon, the ultimate determining condition for the coming-to-be in experience of what is, and can be, for me and for all men. "What is" must conform, as Kant put it, to the transcendental possibilities of experience in general. It is apparent that the ground of this necessity is itself a contingency—namely, the way the human body is given. In turning to explore the proper mode of the human milieu, we shall not be concerned then with a mere psychology, but with the ground conditions, the fond of the world, within and against which background a truth can stand out. *Esse est percipi,* and hence the phenomenological exploration of the appearing of what appears in perception is fundamental ontology. Indeed, phenomenological philosophy itself is a kind of making be, for in taking explicit, reflective possession of the conditions of perception itself, we envision the fundamental sense of what is—the human existent's most authentic way of making Being be.

Our immediate task then is to grasp the ontological significance of the fact that the givenness of the corps propre's anonymous functions provides the background against which the individual moments of experience must appear, that the world is a human milieu.

GENERALITY Perhaps the problem can best be situated if we consider more closely the exact sense in which what we experience in the world transcends. A world, after all, of its very nature bespeaks an otherness: what happens in the world is in some sense "out there," over against me. Yet we have just come to realize that, from the transcendental viewpoint, the world itself is a lived experience, the horizons of which are grounded in my corps propre. But the corps propre itself must also be in the world whose very possibility it grounds as a noematic general milieu. Properly understood, every moment of experience that appears to me, the concrete, voluntary, reflecting ego, is *my* experience, but at the same time, it escapes my efforts to possess it absolutely and manifests itself as belonging, en soi, to others as well.

The world, as general, transcends the ego. The context or horizon of world stands as "general" to its "particular," the moment which succeeds in any way in distinguishing itself sufficiently to motivate attention. It does not matter whether the moment be a "thing," "person," "identifiable collectivity or institution," "idea," etc. In every case the fond is general, the figure particular. What we must seek to understand here is the subtle and profound transformation Merleau-Ponty, inspired by the Gestaltists, has brought to the traditional problem of the one and the many.[10] The general background or context (fond) attaches the particular present configuration of this thing or moment to both the relevant preceding (in either a spatial or temporal sense) experience and to the relevant experience to come, thereby assuring that it has a sense.[11] An absolutely isolated moment that did not refer, because it could not be attached to anything else, would not mean anything, would have no sense. The figure, which has to be different in order to be distinguished, still has to be relevant to a universe of discourse. This relationship of the figure to the spatial-temporal background which gives it sense is more fundamental than the relationship of a particular thing to the general essence it exemplifies. From Greek philosophy until the time of Hegel, philosophers have failed to push deeply enough to that primordial moment when the particular instance gets its sense from the whole context.

To illustrate this primordial relationship, consider the simple ex-

10. Husserl distinguishes the *Innenhorizont*, which links the present *Abschattung* (profile or aspect) to all previous or future possible holds I may have on the same thing, and the *Aussenhorizont*, which links it to the *Mitobjeckten*, all the other things (*Erfahrung und Urteil*, para. 8.) In the same text he speaks of the Horizons as permitting an induction into the particular experience itself and there suggests that that makes possible induction in the more familiar sense. Merleau-Ponty's development of the notion of a corporeally grounded mode of generality, which we are seeking in these pages to systematize out of the manifold allusions, suggestions, and implications the *Phenomenology* offers us, exploits Husserl's precious insight to the full.

11. A recently published "working note" has since come to my attention, in which Merleau-Ponty writes (Nov. 1959): "Generality of things: why are there several examples of the same thing? This is imposed by the very definition of things as beings of a field: How could there be field without generality?" *VI*, p. 273.

ample of my perception of a red splotch on the carpet as part of its intended design. Presumably the splotch has a sufficient structure in itself to motivate my attention to dwell on it. But if I grasp its sense as part of the design, I must be able to experience the splotch as a moment in a whole, a total pattern, within which all of the individual splotches receive their proper meaning. The design as a whole is general in relationship to any one of the splotches.

To consider the example of the splotch within the rug's design as a merely spatial one would be to miss an essential dimension of Merleau-Ponty's existentialization of the one-many experience. There are several senses in which we can think of the whole context of the design as coming before and continuing after the individual splotch. There is the sense in which my previous experiences of pattern operate in the present instance as a general preparation for my grasp-ing the sense of *this* pattern. Moreover, my present experience of this pattern strengthens the general habit and therefore will facilitate my future seizing upon the sense of patterns. But even in the present experience, there is a kind of before and after. Merleau-Ponty likes to emphasize the need to scan the complex whole, and in the process of the eye's running over the design, we are to think of its retaining what it has seen a moment ago and its anticipating what it is going to see a minute from now. In addition to the spatial and temporal dimension of the generality of experience there is a third dimension, its intersubjectivity. Here we should recall what has been said of the corps propre's anonymous functions. We can perceive an inter-subjective world because we possess the same kind of body, capable of the same generality as those of the other subjects, for all of our bodies open into a common world in the same style. The general milieu thus furnished makes possible the grasp of approximately the same object by several existents, although each perceives from a different point of view.[12] It is because each subject's field is not an individual subjective possession but rather is itself made up of the

12. "In reality the Other is not enclosed in my perspective on the world because that perspective itself has no definite limits, (rather) it slides spon-taneously into that of the other and they are gathered up [*recueillies*] together in a single world in which we all participate as anonymous subjects of percep-tion." *PP*, p. 406.

general stuff which becomes the background of the object's very meaning when grasped by a human comportment—as "thing," "idea," "institution," or "expression"—that the interlacing of intentional fields is possible. The relationship between my present grasp of a given perceptual object and my previous and future grasps of the same object is identical with the relationship between my present grasp of the object from my point of view and the manifold grasps other persons experience within their situations in time and space (*PP*, p. 390). Again, both are identical to the relationship between the object upon which attention is focused and its context of other surrounding objects, its world. In all three instances the relationship is one of creative (*PP*, p. 415), dialectical coexistence, of synchrony.[13] By thus appealing to a perceptual horizon furnished by corporeal comportment, by thus pointing out the generality of the experience's unity as contrasted with the particularity of this figure belonging to a moment in time and a position in space, Merleau-Ponty can solve both the problem of the object's transcending the cogito (in the sense of the explicit grasp of this figure at this moment) and the problem of the intersubjectivity of that objectivity. At the same time the groundwork is prepared for a theory of finite freedom.[14]

The replacement of earlier formulations of the one-many relationship by the dialectic of figure-background results in the transformation of what was conceived as a stable relationship into a dynamic one. In the kind of tense equilibrium which exists between figure and background, the alteration of one element, bringing about as it does a shift in the experience's norm or center, inevitably alters its sense.

To illustrate this, let us turn again to basic psychological experiments: In a given perceptual situation, the general *éclairage*—the illumination of the whole spectacle—establishes a kind of norm from which the individual color values receive their sense by functioning as so many deviations from the norm. This norm can be

---

13. This fundamental belief in the world, Merleau-Ponty, following Husserl, terms *Urdoxa*, *PP*, p. 50; cf. *Ideen*, I, pp. 215–16.

14. In *Erfahrung und Urteil*, para. 23, Husserl shows the need to reconceive the notions "passivity-activity" for each kind of experience. Merleau-Ponty has followed his lead in deeply renewing these tired categories of epistemology.

altered by changes either in the objective or in the subjective pole of the perception experience. If a piece of white paper is introduced into the beam of an arc light focused on a disk, the beam, which until then was confounded with the disk on which it was falling to form a unified luminous cone, is now dissociated from the disk and stands out for the first time as illumination (*PP*, p. 360). The introduction of a new value disaggregates the old unity and calls for reorganization of the sense of the whole lived spectacle. Similarly, when a package of typewriter paper is spread across my desk so that some of the pieces lie in deep shadow and others directly under the lamp, I can, by deliberately suspending my unreflecting spontaneous movement into the spectacle, be brought to admit that the white values of the deeply shaded and those of the brightly lit pieces are not objectively the same. I spontaneously live all the pieces of paper as equivalent in color value, but my reflective act can alter the spectacle's presentation.

The same unstable equilibrium is evident on a higher plane, in a widely different sphere of intentional activity: language. The general sense of the words I use in discourse—their ability to fit into an infinity of contexts—receives its particular determination by the position the words assume in the present context. The relationship of the context to the particular words is general, but the generality of each word (the wide range of possible meanings of its constellation of sounds) is brought down to a particular meaning by its place in the context, and it is the particularity-generality of the words that establishes the context. The sense in which the particular meaning is a deviation from a norm—the general range of possible sense the words, thanks to their sedimented history, bring with them—is here fairly palpable.

The dialectical tension between moment and background stands out clearly in these examples: If the norm is altered, the sense of all the moments will be shifted; shift the moments and the change will be felt throughout the constellation of givens that are grouped within the horizons of a given lived configuration. Such descriptions from the transcendental viewpoint emphasize the lived nature—we might say the organic unity—of experience. We begin to realize that whatever sort of an initiative is introduced into such a scheme, whether an act of initiative on the part of the active subject or a point of initiative introduced by a sensible given, it necessarily brings about alteration of the global scene; and the new element must struggle against all the resistances that were previously populating the field of experience.

One feels at once the limitless implications looming up when no moment within experience can be regarded as an isolated en soi, when every point of newness must achieve a place for itself by de-centering and recentering the dynamic unity of the field of experience, when the moment of experience—be it stimulus in a constellation of stimuli, thing in a landscape, word in a sentence, individual in a class, or institution in a nation—can exercise a leverage on the whole just as every alteration of the whole changes the sense of the moment. In such circumstances, the liberty exercised by any sort of initiative within a field must have its limits: every initiative must struggle against the generalized resistance of the whole and must derive its very sense from that resisting totality. All the traditional formulations of philosophy envisioning a relationship between a lower (concrete, sensible) and a higher (universal, intellectual) moment of experience must then be rethought in the more dynamic terms of this funda-mental dialectic, and, consequently, the pretenses of reason to pro-nounce absolutely—i.e. to achieve a generality no longer subject to the moments' becoming—must be reconsidered in the light of the dialectic of our perceptual insertion in the world.

Now that the first outlines of the philosophy into which such con-siderations will lead us have begun to become apparent, there remains the question of where we can best begin to describe in detail the actual dialectic between general fond and particular figure that is the very development of experience and the source of the world's history. Let us follow Husserl's example, taking the course of a natural genetic.

THE FILLING UP OF EMPTY HORIZONS: ATTENTION Be-cause I am born with the corps propre I am given an initial and fundamental opening-into-the-world. This is the original situation Heidegger describes as *Geworfenheit,* thrownness. Merleau-Ponty conceives this initial pact signed with the world "without my com-plicity —that is, without experience-actualizing initiatives—as "minimal"; it provides "only a sketchy outline of a veritable presence in the world" (*PP*, p. 193) and requires those conscious attentive acts in order to fill up (in the sense of the Husserlian *Erfüllung*)[15] with the articulated objects of adult perception. It is important to realize that we can discover in our experience here and now that natural fond, that *pré-histoire,* which provides the ultimate horizons and first ground for all our subsequent history, as a significant text makes clear:

> Through the sensation I seize on the margin of my personal life and my own acts a *given* life of consciousness from which they emerge, the life of my eyes, of my hands, of my ears, which are so many natural "I's." Each time I experience a sensation, I experience that it interests not my own particular being, that for which I am responsible and about which I can decide, but another me which has already opted for the world, which has already opened itself up to certain of its aspects and synchronized itself with them. Between my sensation and me, there is always the thickness of a *primordial* acquisition which keeps my experience from being clear for itself (*PP*, p. 250).

The suggestion that subsequent cultural experience is grounded in the primordial acquisition, the cultural-historical in the natural world, will help to situate all "mythic" spaces in relation to "real" intellectual space by reference to the given natural fond which shows through in the analysis of the child's or the primitive's experience as "the canvas shows through the painting." Moreover, it throws light on psychopathology by partially explaining how the disturbed person's cultural world can disintegrate without necessarily destroying his entire hold on the natural space, which nevertheless, is clearly not normally filled up. But more important than either of these significant aspects is the suggestion that the very reality of our liberty lies in whatever may be the possibilities of dialogue between these levels and between the moments within the backgrounds these levels provide.[16]

15. *Ideen* I, para. 138b, 140, 141, 145b.
16. The later essays make clearer than the *Phenomenology* the extent to which the distinction between "natural" and "cultural-historical" must, in a

In order to grasp those possibilities, two notions are essential: the master dialectic between the ego (as center of initiative in the giving-of-a-sense) and the givens (the already-filled horizons out of which the initiative both grows and upon which it must impose a new orientation, a new sense) must be understood; and, concurrently, all the levels of our experience interior to that master structure must be seen to interrelate dialectically. Consideration of the act of attend-ing, the most basic intentional initiative a subject can take in order to fill up the horizons offered to him and thus to provide himself with a perceptual object, will clarify on the most fundamental level the very nature of the intentional subject's institution of a sense.

Attention is not a formal, independent initiative without roots, but, on the contrary, a possibility that is itself given initially in the form of an empty intention—i.e. as general horizon (which itself is not nothing) interior to which it will be possible to determine and interpret a certain figure (*PP,* p. 36 ff.). The act of attention is a kind of gathering up of the proffered dispersed and indetermined pos-sibilities in order to form the figure. It is *l'aménagement d'un certain espace mental.* Psychologists have long known that, during the first nine months, an infant can distinguish only grossly the colored and the achromatic; he later develops the ability to articulate the colored expanses into warm shades and cold shades and then finally begins distinguishing the details of the different colors. Since until recently psychologists could not represent to themselves a perceptual field in which there are no determined colors of the sort which populate the more articulated adult perception, they simply concluded that infants saw colors but didn't know their names. This was a failure to understand the essentially creative nature of attention. They failed to see that attending is not simply illuminating more completely existent givens but is achieving a new articulation by transforming

---

transcendental philosophy, be one of degree rather than kind. Indeed, as we shall see in due course, the inability to distinguish effectively a fond of nature beneath the long accumulations of history leads to serious difficulties, com-promising the possibility of grounding an objective theory of truth and leaving the dialectic referred to here both ultimately anchorless. But these are critical considerations which we must leave for later.

horizons into figures (*PP*, p. 38[17]). Attention is "the active constitution of a new object which explicates and thematizes what was offered until then only as indeterminate horizons" (*PP*, p. 39). The object presents itself as still indeterminate possibility; it motivates the consciousness to take up what is still only ambiguous; with the help of the generalized resources of his sedimented experience of the world, the subject is able to determine the amorphous given into his object. Correlatively, prior to the act of attention, the indetermination, the generality of the subject's horizons offer a range of possibility—Merleau-Ponty speaks in this context of a "liberty of indetermination"—which he must momentarily alienate in responding as he does to the ambiguous solicitations of the object; for when the subject gives himself an actual determined object, he directs and engages himself, forming its own personal history. This bipolar liberty of indetermination, man's capacity to direct the course of the determination, implies a certain *recul* vis-à-vis the sensible givens. "This passage from the indetermined to the determined, this *reprise* at every instant of its own history in the unity of a new sense, this is thought itself" (*PP*, p. 39). Merleau-Ponty cites Valéry: "The work of the spirit exists only in act."[18]

Envisioned here is a given which is not an absolutely determined *en soi* but a solicitation within a range of possibility, just as a particular word can be considered an invitation to a certain range of possible expressive comportments. Such an empty intention is empty but not nothing; it is *un creux* (a depression) *dans l'être*, not a *trou* (a hole) but a *vide déterminé*. It invites filling up, but the act of taking it up is not the act of an absolute Ego, capable of anything and of making anything out of anything. Rather, the attending subject acts as an existent possessed of a generalized history, founded in the natural horizons provided by the body's original givenness, and further empowered by the sedimented, habitual, generalized horizons of interpretation accumulated during his personal history, "the cultural body." When I listen to a discourse, the words do not determine my act of comprehension absolutely (if that were so, all the auditors would understand in the same fashion) but rather solicit

17. Merleau-Ponty cites Koffka.
18. *Introduction à la poétique*, p. 40.

the deployment of my general possibilities of interpretation. If the listener cannot speak the speaker's language, if a child is listening to a theologian's discourse, or if a Barthian is listening to a Dominican, the response to the solicitation may fall far short of actualizing the best potentialities that are held out by the pronounced words. It must be noted, however, that no absolute understanding of discourse is possible, least of all by the speaker himself, for the words drag with them endless general worlds. Thus the criticism of a piece of literature is never ended, the implications of a statement are never exhausted.

Similarly, because the infant cannot respond to the solicitation of the colors, no shades of color as the adult experiences them appear in his phenomenal field. Only when the corps propre is physiologically prepared to deploy a new a priori does the finer articulation become possible. The difference between the corps propre's deployment of a priori and the subject's giving of a sense out of the resources of his personal history lies in the greater range, the flexibility, the greater degree of willful initiative the corps propre is able, in the last case, to exercise over the instruments provided by the full human comportment.

The Command of Space-Time as Ground of Our Liberty

CONTRAST WITH HIGHER ANIMALS A brief sketch of Merleau-Ponty's contrast of human comportment with the less flexible possibilities of the higher animals, as developed in *The Structure of Behavior,* may serve to emphasize this last, important point. At the same time, it will provide a wider perspective on the concept that freedom is bound up with the power to meet the givens of one's situation with a maximum of interpretative range.

When Wilhelm Koehler set up some rather natural problems for bright chimpanzees to solve by using evermore complicated instruments, he reached one conclusion easily: the ape structures his milieu much more exclusively than the human being in terms of lines of force that stretch rather rigidly out from his body. When an ape sought to reach outside of his cage for bananas using proffered pieces of bamboo that could be fitted together to form a pole, he arrived quickly at the solution if the pieces were laid in a straight line stretching along his line of vision toward the fruit. When the sticks were placed at random, the solution was usually discovered by accident, when the animal happened to bring the sticks into line after trying every sort of possibility and configuration. Similarly, when several boxes could be piled on top of one another to reach bananas hanging from the top of the cage, the ape showed no immediate grasp of a possible relationship between the scattered boxes or of the importance of the relative size of the boxes. His first tendency was to pick up a box and wave it vaguely toward the fruit or to push any object in that general direction (including, on one occasion, the hapless keeper). When he had finally groped to the correct solution, he scrambled up his pile and, with incredible acrobatics, reached for the fruit. Koehler remarks that the pile of boxes, instead of being conceived of as a stable platform, was apparently seen as an extension of the ape's own body, as though he felt the lines of force passing through the teetering mass which he managed to keep in precarious equilibrium just long enough to solve his problem.

One thing then is apparent: The ape shows little talent for imagining the situation from the thing's point of view, from "over there." When, in a now classic experiment, the bananas were placed in a three-sided box outside but up against the cage with the open side away from the bars, the solution was obvious—to any adult human being: reach out with a stick, push the fruit away so that it will slide out of the box, and then pull it back through the bars. But the ape, it seems, had great trouble projecting himself, so to speak, into the fruit's point of view. He kept trying to pull the fruit to himself immediately until he finally solved the problem more or less by accident, a wild blow of the stick having sent the bananas flying out of the box. The same ape who had been able to project himself rapidly and unfailingly through a complicated maze to get at the sighted object could barely learn to push the fruit itself through even the simplest maze. Apparently, only with great difficulty could he disengage himself from his real spatial position and identify himself with the thing to be maneuvered.

The suggestion that human superiority consists in greater freedom to survey the structure within the perceptual field and thus command much more creatively the range of time and space it opens reinforces

Merleau-Ponty's main point. If our properly human capabilities are rooted in that liberty of indifference, which offers us a certain leeway in focusing attention and thus in structuring the phenomenal field, the time-space relations with which we are bound up are not those rigid ones of the animal; to the inevitable flow of events we can oppose more than instinct. Our attentive acts, says Merleau-Ponty, borrowing Husserl's language once again, permit us *überzuschauen*—to dominate —the situation. Deeper-lying natural time and space show through our more creative superimpositions, as we shall shortly learn, but the human existent, as ego, is able to transcend the originally given structures and thus to gather up moments and assemble worlds through the power termed "symbolization." A sense-giver who actualizes, instead of the rigid instinctive forms of the animal, the generalized possibility of the cultural body—of a history; who is able to build upon nature a creative human world structured with signs is an existent; he is able to live the paradox of a finite freedom. It is the nature of his superior comportment—the existential-space-opening act of an ego capable of transcending the nature in which it is rooted—that we must seek to describe.

NOT SPACE BUT SPACES, FOLLOWING THE DIFFERENT MODES OF OUR "FIXATION DANS LE MONDE" Because the animal's body is different, his space is not like the human's. Even within human space, as we have suggested, there is reason to distinguish the more fundamental natural space (that given with préhistoire as the very frame of our *Geworfenheit,* the initial being-in-the-world which comes with our bodily endowment) and other spaces, more particular *paysages,* such as those distinguishing the child's from the adult's world. The notion of comportmental space can obviously englobe every sort of relation with an object (the space of traditional geometry being merely one sort, which itself of course has to be related to the others). The essential problem is how man can enjoy any distance at all from objects of various sorts—not only sensible things but mythical entities, artistic worlds, the landscape of discourse, etc.—that distance which is necessary to make possible their standing "over there" in opposition to me. Such space-opening, as the previous experiments suggested, is the very ground of transcendence both of the object in its otherness and of the ego as center of initiative not so absorbed by the experience that it is incapable of dominating it in some way.

The study of this primordial space-opening which keeps the objects at just the distance necessary for our normal handling of them, i.e. neither so far as to leave us untouched, nor so close as to obsess us, is normally hampered by our absorption in the results of all our constitutive activity, that is, by the things with which our practical projects deal. Once again, we must cast about for an unusual experience that will provide a glimpse of the activity at work precisely when its fully, we might say properly, constituted objects are not there.

In the darkest of nights, the world of clear and articulated objects is abolished, but our perceptive being, although "amputated" from its world, nevertheless goes on opening a space without things. The night itself is no object standing over against me; rather "it envelops me, penetrating all the sense, suffocating my memory, almost effacing my personal identity." I am no longer confined to the perceptive post from which I customarily see the profiles of things file by at a distance, for the dark has no profiles. It touches me immediately and enjoys an almost mystical unity.[19] Even a cry or a distant light populate it only vaguely, seem to animate it all at once; it is a pure depth without planes, without surfaces, without distance between me and it. At the opposite pole from geometric space, which seems borne up and tied together by thought and which itself seems to be working from no particular place, nocturnal space appears to radiate from me as its center. Anguish lurks in the night because experiencing the night is experiencing the primordial space-opening act; it brings us face to face with our contingency, the gratuitous and untiring movement by which we seek to anchor ourselves in and transcend toward fixed, definite things, without any guarantee of always finding them there (PP, p. 328).

19. Merleau-Ponty is describing here the primordial encounter, the oneness of body and world, before the objectivizing acts fix and étalent their objects. In S, an effort will be made to make us aware that this primordial closeness remains underneath the distances established by the ek-sistential acts; in those pages we shall see for instance that the other person and I "haunt" the same space.

Even in the dark, however, I can still utilize, as I grope for example through my apartment, the general montage made familiar to me by use throughout the day; I can keep referring mentally to my knowledge of where and what things are. Moreover, the night is still a fact of nature, and there is something reassuring and even terrestrial in its blackness. A more striking instance where we begin to appreciate the body's active contribution (*reel,* in Husserl's sense) to the structuring of space can be found in sleep and dreams. When I hold the world off at a distance and turn in sleep toward the subjective sources of my existence, there surges up the most general of spaces, the deepest and least articulated. In dreaming, a corporeal fact such as breathing or sexual desire may polarize my entire psychic activity, becoming infused by it with general significance. The resulting dream is structured as a spatial image, but the space follows its own, fully alogical rules—"a great bird hovering which, hit by a bullet, suddenly falls and shrivels up into a little heap of blackened paper." What is the relation between the physical fact that triggered off the dream and the structured image? More important, what is the relation between the physical space in which the feeling occurred, the intellectual space in which the elements of the dream were gathered, and the dream theater in which the image took place? Certainly it is not narrowly symbolic, like that between a stop sign and the presence of an intersection. The dream does not merely stand for the fact's intrinsic meaning, any more than myths or poetic images merely stand for anything extrinsic. Neither is that relation simply one of analogy. The corporeal fact and the dream image are equivalent as similar expressions of a direction of our existence; the three spaces are equivalent as expressions of the essential being-in-the-world that makes this existence possible.

Whatever can be discovered about how one lives a space is revealing of the total life of that subject, "of the energy with which he tends toward a future through his body and through his world" (*PP,* p. 327). If I say, "my expectations grew higher," I am not describing some obscure law of the mechanics of my nervous system or simply comparing my feeling with the sort of growth found in nature or comparing this upward movement with the gesture of reaching for a desired object. The movement upward in space and that of desire toward its object can be symbolically related because they both express the same essential structure of our being as one situated in respect to a milieu—i.e. related to dynamic, limiting contingencies—whose finitude alone gives any sense to the directions "high" and "low." When one speaks of a low or an elevated morality, one is not simply extending into the psychic realm a relationship whose full sense exists only in the physical world; rather one is utilizing, in the words of the existentialist psychologist Binswanger, "a direction of significance which, so to speak, traverses the different regional spheres and receives in each a particular signification (spatial, auditory, spiritual, psychic, etc.)."[20] The big bird that soars and then falls, disintegrating into a heap of cinders, does not do so in a physical space but rather rises and falls with the existential tide in me—it is a form of the pulsation of my existence. Just as in waking life my commerce with the world as it proposes itself determines a space for realities, so when I am asleep the existential tide at each moment determines a space of phantasms (PP, p. 330)

These examples indicate that the surge of existence continues to radiate a space even when the conditions, whether external (the night) or corporeal (in sleep or in mental illness, should the corporeal schema be troubled), are unusual. In such abnormal situations, that activity is more obvious. But even when the normal objective world has been spread before us by the spontaneous activity of the corps propre, evidences of the existential spatial surge can be found at work beneath the more fixed, explicit things at the center of awareness. A moment's reflection suffices to make us realize that our normal, waking world is shot through with mythic spaces similar to the space of dreams, "spaces in which the directions and positions are determined by the residence of the great affective entities" (PP, p. 330).

20. L. Binswanger, *Traum und Existenz*, p. 674, cited *PP*, p. 329. Students of the history of the debates, conflicts, and cooperations between the existentialist psychologists, the Freudians, and the existentialist phenomenologists will have recognized already the traces of Binswanger's influence in these pages of the *Phenomenology*. For a brief, intelligible introduction to this important aspect of phenomenology, which, because of our more exclusively philosophical (ontologico-epistemic) concerns we have not endeavored to bring out, see A. Hesnard, *L'Œuvre de Freud*, esp. Chapter 8, *"Psychanalyse et Philosophie."*

The location and nature of the phenomenon in the dream or the myth depend on the directions of our desires, on what we fear, on what we feel our lives dependent upon. When the primitive man finds his campsite inhabited by friendly gods, the forest by menacing demons, and the raindrops by fertile spirits, his infantile myth is not radically different from the affectivity that structures my own existential geography. While on vacation, I may easily come to share the local farmers' anxiety about the exceptional drought, but if I open the paper and learn that war is menacing, I suddenly feel exiled in this village, far from the center of things. Most ordinary space is thus neither fully real nor fully imaginary; it is filled with affective content. When, as in mental illness, it loses much of that content, things appear as empty shells, mere vestiges of what they were.

The lived distance between a person and things holds the measure at each moment of the amplitude and normalcy of his life. Ordinarily, space permits our accustomed domination of things and thus keeps them at the right distance for the customary practical dealings we, as plain, sophisticated adults, are used to carrying out with them. In normal space, we are neither indifferent to things nor unduly possessed by any of them. The surge of mythical space is then able to compose smoothly with the natural space intersubjectively inhabited by all the other existents. What is past, for instance, usually slips away into general sedimentation; in contrast, the disturbed person's complex is a moment that has failed to move along with the usual flow of a human history and that now obstructs the present by structuring the phenomenal field abnormally, shifting all values.

Disturbance becomes intense when private space takes over, when the subject becomes incapable of the normal automatic insertion into our common natural space. A schizophrenic, for example, may be fascinated by a given sight, such as a mountain landscape, for example. Suddenly, he feels a foreign force snatch the landscape from him; he sees a second sky, black and limitless, penetrate the blue evening. This empty, invisible, terrifying sky is for a moment only part of the autumnal landscape, but then the earth itself seems absorbed by it. All the time, declares the sick man, "a permanent question is being asked me, like an order to go get some rest or to die or to go farther." This second space traversing the visible space is that of the general projection of the world, and the schizophrenic's difficulty, according to Merleau-Ponty, results from the dissociation of this perpetual projection from the objective world as it is given in the present spectacle. The fundamental projection is no longer completely absorbed by the task of affectively animating the landscape of the moment; the schizophrenic no longer lives in the common world. He remains in the landscape's space instead of coordinating it to the geographic space, which should normally be structured simultaneously by the corps propre; and the actual landscape, once it has been cut off from the common world, is considerably impoverished. Everything astonishes the victim and turns into a question; the world no longer goes without saying, for his world-projecting power, lacking its normal energy, is unable to fill the moment with sense, to make it equivalent to every other possible moment of existence.[21] The contingency of the world-projecting power and thus his own and the thing's contingency begins to show through. "If the natural space of which classical psychology speaks is, in contrast to this, reassuring and evident, it is because existence rushes in and loses itself in it" (*PP*, p. 332).

Hallucinations and private myths are a shriveling up of the lived space: space is no longer structured in a way that keeps the object at a distance sufficient to permit dealing with it in the fashion we are accustomed to in our daily commerce with things. Even when a schizophrenic feels that a brush laid down near his window has come up to him and entered his head, he may nevertheless know that the brush is "over there."[22] But the brush "over there" has become a mere phantom, because the true brush, the rigid and prickly being, has left the window and become stuck in his head. That solidarity of man and world which the phenomenology of intentionality has rediscovered, that intimacy of noesis and noema which is always there in our everyday experience but is usually structured properly,

21. The case is reported by F. Fischer, *Raum-Zeitstrucktur und Denkstörung in der Schizophrenie*, p. 253, cited *PP*, p. 332.

22. L. Binswanger, *Das Raumproblem in der Psychopathologie*, p. 630, cited *PP*, p. 336.

has been altered; insufficient room has been left between the perceiver and the perceived, thus impeding the customary smooth existential flow of properly related spatial layers.

A further question now arises: which is the true space—our
natural, clear, objective space or the anthropological spaces discovered
in myths, dreams, and hallucinations? The intellectualist philosopher
(like the average adult, the civilized, commonsense man) simply
writes off such odd experiences as psychological curiosities. By re-
garding them as devoid of any important philosophical significance,
he is left free to deduct a single space that is suitable for a world
where all things can be thought and where the truth must be both
univocal and omnipresent. As we have seen, however, even our
normally lived natural space has little in common with the unequivocal
ideal of Euclidean geometry. Moreover, to dismiss myths and hallucinations is to overlook the significant fact that the primitive and the
child really believe their myths (just as I really believe that there is a
big flat rock in my path until I draw closer and only then realize
that it is just a bright patch of sunlight). Now the final test of any
theory of truth must be its ability to account for all phenomena,
especially the phenomenon of error. If such breaches can somehow
be opened in the normal world, it must contain "layers" that can
slide apart to permit the illusion, the dream, the myth to enter the
clear structure of natural space. Such an approach expresses the problem noematically, but we already confronted the same issue noetically
when we asked how our existence could surge ahead of what the
world solicits. The importance of the question, of course, lies in the
fact that our liberty, as we suggested earlier, consists in the initiatives
we are able to take in moving about in our existential spaces.

THE ANTHROPOLOGICAL SPACES PRESUPPOSE THE CON-
STITUTION OF NATURAL SPACE Natural space is often invaded
by anthropological space, "haunted," as Merleau-Ponty once put it,
by hallucination and myth. This expression suggests the precedence
of natural space over all others. Anthropological spaces are constructed on natural space (the nonobjectivizing acts on the objectivizing ones, as Husserl would say) (PP, p. 340[23]). The schizophrenic

23. Merleau-Ponty cites the fifth *Logische Untersuchungen*, pp. 387ff.

knows that the brush is indeed "over there" in natural space, even though he doesn't consider it to be the real brush, the one he can feel. The precedence of natural space is what leads to the common error of conceiving it to be an object of thought devoid of all ambivalence, like geometric space. It must, however, be recognized for what it is: a horizon of possible objectivizations and comportments, a call to be in the world in a certain way. The primitive constructs his mythical space against a background (fond) of natural space that is clearly enough articulated to make possible such acts of everyday life as fishing, hunting, and even relations with civilized men. His mythical space, no matter how diffuse, is a variation on that basic structure; it organizes his world further and calls him to certain attitudes about that world. The sacredness of the campground expresses a relationship between that one place and all other locations; the presence of the god in the rain establishes a rapport with his nonpresence elsewhere.

The mythical consciousness does not objectivize as the familiar consciousness of the thing we explicitly think about. Subjectively, it is always in flux, never becoming very aware of itself; objectively, the object it crystallizes is not defined in clear terms by a certain number of neatly articulated properties. Yet if mythical consciousness were not an effort to structure the world, it would not be consciousness of anything at all. Such a consciousness certainly does not stand at what would be considered a normal distance from its noema, but unless it attempted at least a rudimentary movement of objectivization, it would not crystallize itself in myths at all (PP, p. 338). The interpenetration of spaces—indeed, their very multiplicity—by forcing us to seek the rapports between these spaces, strikingly brings out their ontological significance: it reveals them to be moments of experience that are structured by the existent's form of being-in-the-world, of which they are but the noematic correlates. The primordial space, our natural space, is the original corporeal structure that makes being-in-the-world at all possible. All the others are variations on this basic theme.

Just as the mythical consciousness must build about some nuclei of signification which it takes from its own natural world, so must the dream and the hallucination contain elements of the natural world. The space of the dream may be cut off from the clear space of the waking world, but it makes free use of all its articulations; "The world obsesses us even in sleep; it is on and about the world (*sur le monde*) that we dream" (*PP*, p. 339). Even folly gravitates about the world. This is obvious in the case of morbid reveries which try to fabricate a private domain out of the debris of the world; even in the most severe cases of depression—those in which the sick person, as it were, installs his dwelling place in death—the being of the world is still utilized, for the individual borrows what he needs to structure his denial of it.

Less dramatically, in a familiar experience's fully natural world the anthropologic worlds we mingle with it often show through "as the canvas shows through the painting." If I am walking across the Place de la Concorde, with all of Paris as my field of action, and suddenly fasten my eyes on the stone wall that retains the parapet of the Tuileries, la Concorde (and with it all Paris as that familiar human agglomeration) will disappear. With nothing before me now but a historyless stone, I can restrict my attention still more, until there is only a gray, grainy surface, the play of light on an indefinite matter. While my total perception is of course made up of more than such analytic moments, it can always be dissolved into them. My body, through its habits, can assure my insertion into the cultural, human world, but it must first project me (thanks to the *acquis originaire*) into that natural world, which can thus always be seen to show through. Even perceptions of what is desired by desire, loved by love, or hated by hate always form about sensible nuclei, however scanty; it is in the primary sense data that they seek verification and find fullness.

In summary, although Merleau-Ponty attempted no systematic enumeration of all the possibilities for different kinds of spatiality, depending on the different ways an existent installs himself in the world, he insists that whatever sort of anthropological space there may prove to be is essentially dependent upon the natural space. All the more intellectual and fanciful acts presuppose the corps propre's given, fundamental world-opening. If existence as such is spatial, no human act is without its kind of spatiality, and, correlatively, no opening of a space can occur without employing as its core at least a residue of the natural world. Our intentional acts can thus legitimately be said to transcend because the opening of a space is the act of transcendence itself; it relates a subject to a reality that is other than himself, but against which, as ego, he is able to advance his claims— i.e. which he is able to dominate.

Conversely, of course, "All space is existential."[24] Even Euclidian space is a historical world-structuring, an anthropological variation on spontaneously lived natural space.[25] "Existential" must not be understood here, or elsewhere in Merleau-Ponty, to refer only to the primordial, prepersonal contributions of the corps propre. It applies to all acts that enjoy a general mode because they depend on what has been sedimented in the corps propre—not only the acts establishing the natural world, but all intentional acts reaching through the

24. A very intriguing aspect of this inherent tendency to a sort of dynamic spatiality on the part of any kind of idea we may have is the fact that our systems of ideas unfold in a kind of landscape of their own through which the imagination can wander. In PP, Merleau-Ponty only suggests this in passing, but the phenomenologist's descriptions of an existential-intentional space call for us to recognize its importance, and in Signs the notion comes into its own. Each philosophy has a characteristic "feel." We move about in it as in a familiar spiritual world. I believe we also develop a paysage for our individual conception of history. Certain sensible images may form the nuclei of signification according to which model imaginative lines of movement spread to form the structure of the historical course of events. The affective tone of the images changes as I move from the Middle Ages to the Renaissance. And who is to deny that the eighteenth century forms for me a world, admitting certain kinds of phenomena linked in characteristic ways and bathed in a special "light of reason"? The following text offers a good illustration of a different sort of space, this time an aesthetic one: "One could show, for example, that aesthetic perception opens in its turn a new space, that the painting as work of art is not in the space it inhabits as a physical thing and as a colored canvas, that the dance unfolds in a space without ends and without directions, that it is a suspension of our history, that in the dance the subject and his world are no longer opposed, no longer detach themselves each against the background furnished by the other, that, consequently, the parts of the body are no longer accentuated in the way they are in natural experience: the trunk is no longer the fond from which arise the movements and into which they melt again once achieved; it directs the dance and the movements of the members are at its service." PP, p. 333n.

25. Merleau-Ponty's support for this point will be discussed in Chapter 3.

emotional and the subjective-imaginary, to the explicit, objective-intellectual.

The Appearance of the Thing Within Natural Space: Unity Within a Flow of Profiles

In order to grasp fully the notion that spatialization is the existent's transcending act, more precise descriptions of the primordial opening of a natural space—especially as it appears in its results—must be considered. The descriptions presented here are intended to reveal the existential role of the body in the constitution of the perceptual object emphasizing the bipolar transcendence of an experience essentially rooted in our mode of living it. In other words, what is to be shown to be pour nous will be seen to be, in the very manner in which the corps propre achieves it, en soi and therefore capable of grounding a truth. Thus the ontological impact of the intentional phenomenon par excellence—the corporeally provided fond—will become apparent.

The first merit of the phenomenologist's formulation is historical: it solves elegantly the classical contradictions in the tradition's effort to explain how, out of a series of experiences that present an object from constantly varying perspectives, the human being manages to perceive a thing constant in shape, size, and color. The empirical psychologist enthusiastically emphasizes the fact that a multiplicity of perspectives is possible but fails to make very comprehensible the means whereby, out of these discrete perceptions of different sizes and from different angles, I can derive the notion that a thing itself has a determined size or a definite shape. Simply to affirm that I utilize as standard a certain perspective—for instance, when the thing is directly before me—or a certain distance and then relate the thing's present presentation to the remembered standard as a variation from it, assumes what must be explained: namely, why this privilege?

The intellectualist suggestion at least explains how there can be determined shapes and sizes. Postulate, as Hegel would for instance, that the world forms a system of which my body (as point of view) and things are so many elements; as those elements change position in regard to one another, their position in respect to everything else also changes, but the system itself does not change. Therefore, things are in a sense determined objects because all the possible values of form or size that they can assume in experience are enclosed in the system from the start. What is affirmed in asserting the particular determination of the object is a *facies totius universi* in which is founded the equivalence of all its apparitions and hence the identity of its being. But this solution simply shifts the problem. In asserting that size and shape are determined by the variations of distance and orientation according to a constant law, the intellectualist is assuming that these qualities can be treated as variable and therefore can be measured. But this implies that somehow they are already determined as though we were able to command the system of which they are part. As such a bird's-eye view is out of the question, the problem of knowing how they become so remains unsolved (*PP,* pp. 346–47).

The psychologist is fond of pointing out that the view of an object one hundred yards away is not the same as the view of the same object ten feet away, but he fails to see the exact nature of that difference and what it indicates about the existential ground of the unity of all perceptions in objective knowledge of identical things. It is a simple but singularly significant fact—and one, incidentally, that enjoys the honor of having once been pointed out by Pascal—that for every object, just as for every painting in the museum, there is an optimal distance from which it is best seen and an optimal orienta tion from which angle it yields itself up most completely to observa-tion. In the best focus, the thing's parts appear in all their articula-tions; when I am either too far away or too close, the parts run together or flee in every direction. A living body looked at through a magnifying glass presents a lunar landscape so strange to the un-familiar eye that the observer does not know how to comprehend it; when seen from far away, the same body loses its animation and be-comes a tiny doll lost in the wider landscape.

The thing yields up more of itself when a certain equilibrium of the interior and exterior horizons is attained; the point of mature understanding is achieved as a kind of dialectical balance between the exigencies of the thing and the possibilities of the body. This optimal range of perception is not simply one among many possible perspectives, but rather the expression of the fullest existential hold this kind of perceiver can have on this kind of thing. It thus becomes the principle of unity for the whole gamut of possible perceptions, the type, as it were, toward which all the other perspectives converge (*PP*, p. 348). Because of my knowledge of its type, as a thing goes farther away or comes closer, instead of perceiving primarily a change in size, I experience a kind of tension oscillating about the norm. If a thing is turned at an odd angle, perception of it is experienced as a disequilibrium, for its influences on me are unequally distributed. If I see a dot high in the sky, then later perceive that it has grown into an airplane, still later into a large transport, and finally into a C–130 turboprop military transport, the individual glimpses seem to be steps toward the grasp of the real plane in its objective size and shape. Perceptions themselves may thus be seen as so many moments in a single gesture leading to the optimal attitude. The unification is existential, and the result transcendent as it yields "the objective size and shape of the thing" (*PP*, pp. 349–50).

The sense in which a perception can be said to be optimal must be understood in the light of our earlier remarks about the teleology of perception. To speak of an equilibrium between the given *montage à l'égard du monde* with which the body opens onto the perceived world and the solicitations of the data inevitably suggests that the things perceived are making their demands, but we pointed out earlier that they must not be conceived as a reality *en soi* to which a comportment—itself imagined as having no effect on the sense of the perception—simply must conform. The montage we now see determines the very conditions of the solicitation or at least the limits within which it can occur. Neither perceiver nor perceived is the preferred determiner, however, for both retain their identity within the transcendent dialectic. The perception is not foreign to the perceiver but is dependent upon him for its being (the supreme sign of this is that we are free to make something out of our world), but neither is the perceived thing simply swallowed up in the ideal world of an absolute transcendental ego. We might even say that the perceiver is for the sake of the perceived, since he is only insofar as he exists in a real world—i.e. as he responds to a milieu of resistances and solicitations which make demands on him that he go on perpetuating them in some form or other.

In a very subtle analysis of illumination, Merleau-Ponty reinforces all these points, showing that within the noema itself we can find indications that the perceiving act is in a sense teleologically geared to the perceived. For example, I may sometimes be aware of definite characteristics of certain types of light, but usually light goes about its task of illuminating without being noticed itself. When I am standing in the sun, the shade looks like shadows, but after I have been in the deep shade a few minutes, I cease to be aware of it as anything but light. When I come in from outside at night, a room lit by fluorescent light seems blue, glaring, and disagreeable; after a few minutes it strikes me as normal. If the twilight comes into the room that is brightly lit by artificial light, it has a greyish color that would not be noticed outdoors. As the particular qualities of light tend to disappear through familiarization, all the objects lit up by it parcel out among themselves the colors of the spectrum according to the degree and mode of their resistance to its atmosphere. As in all our experiences with the functioning of fonds, a norm or level is established through the interplay of bodily montage and appearances as I start to live in the dominant atmosphere, and all the color values that depend on the niveau are redistributed on the objects in function of this fundamental convention. The word "convention" is most appropriate here, since it conveys the body's forming a pact with the appearances—which itself emphasizes the body's active contribution—and the notion of something familiar—of a habitus older than even our first act of perception.

A photograph or a painting may make illumination stand out so much that attention is called to it as a kind of thing itself; for example, in a film showing the exploration of a cave with a lamp, the light, instead of reaching out immaterially to penetrate the darkness and make things appear, tends to solidify as it runs along a wall, becoming a thick blob that blinds the viewer as it spreads over the surface of the screen, competing with things instead of underscoring them (PP, p. 357). Because the film does not do the corps propre's job properly, the light fails to efface itself so that it can carry out its task of leading our gaze to the things.

David Katz in his Aufbau der Farbwelt speaks of this essential function of the illumination as Lichtführung. Merleau-Ponty's explanation strongly underscores this feeling of movement. As light guides me through the spectacle, it helps me make sense out of what is unfolding before me. Even the most static example retains this feeling: If I am alone in a theater when the curtain goes up on a stage set that is brilliantly illumined, "it seems to me that the spectacle is itself visible [transcendence again] or ready to be seen, and that the light which searches through the planes, sketches out the shadows and penetrates the spectacle from end to end realizes before us a sort of vision. Reciprocally our own vision does not do any more than to take on itself and continue the investment of the spectacle by following the paths traced out for it by the illumination (*PP,* p. 358). When the process is seen as so thoroughly dynamic, it is not difficult to imagine that the spectator can take up the movement according to the leads offered and energize the spectacle until it stands before him, dances with him in the full glory of its sense.

Merleau-Ponty uses a very significant comparison here. "We perceive according to the light [*d'après la lumière*] the way we conceive following what the other person says in verbal communication." (The *d'après* has the double sense of "according to" and "after": he has to speak before I know what to think about what he is trying to say, but once he has spoken, it is I who think.) "And just as communication requires a certain *montage linguistique* through which a sense inhabits the words, so perception supposes in us an apparatus capable of answering to the solicitations of the light according to their sense [that is to say, both their direction and their signification, which are one and the same], to concentrate the sparse visibility to achieve what is only just sketched [*ébauché*] in the spectacle" (*PP,* p. 358).

It is easy to see that in the perception of the cultural object the perceiver must bring to the words or the splotches of paint on the canvas a good part of their perceived sense; the objective sound and sight are the occasion for the experience sedimented in my cultural body to fairly effortlessly deploy itself as I move through the discourse or peruse the canvas. A similar process can be discovered in the body's movement through the natural spectacle, and the comparison of perception to language indicates the full impact of the declaration that the world is woven out of the texture of the body. What is here and now concretely sensed is only the *ébauche* of the full perception I actually enjoy because I am capable of gathering up the sparse sense that is offered and of fleshing it out with experience the corps propre is able to deploy according to that science of the world which is built into the *montage à l'égard du monde*.[26] The meaningful gaze (*le regard*) capable of grasping the sense of the spectacle is the result of the dialectical union, "the natural correlation of the appearance and our kinesthetic unwindings, not known in a law, but lived as the engagement of our body in the typical structures of a world," in other words, as I mentioned earlier, a kind of dance.

The Unity of the Substance and the Fullness of the World

The Phenomenology of Perception analyzes and explains in detail phenomena of constancy for all the senses, but its major philosophical points have already been made clear. Constancy of color, shape, size, or any other quality is simply an abstract moment of the constancy of things which, in turn (like the constancy of every one of the moments), is founded in the total comportment of the body reaching out to found a world. The body is fundamentally intentional, since every moment of its life is striving to found a consistent world by seeking to harmonize that moment with every other moment. Husserl's *Urdoxa* can now be understood simply as the expression of the prime effect of that intentional body which we are given and which manifests itself, declares Merleau-Ponty, as a spontaneous *parti-pris en faveur de l'être*, a presumption of unity and consistency.

The kernel of Merleau-Ponty's ontology is contained in this notion, but before we explore its implications, let us note its cogency in the present context. As the existent strives to achieve the unity of the world by integrating all its perceptions into a total grasp of constant things, regulated as it is "by a logic which assigns each object its determinations in function of all the others," all aberrant givens—those that cannot be configurated, as they will not integrate smoothly with the others—are simply "crossed out" as unreal (*PP*, p. 361). Similarly, when a phenomenon does not resist the corps propre suffi-

26. Recall that the schizoid's world is so empty because something is preventing his deploying with full energy all the body's resources, which leaves him with little more than what is actually sensibly imposing itself.

ciently to demand a configuration of its own, it becomes contaminated by the structures nearest it and can hardly be called "a thing." The sky, for example, is so thin and so distant at the horizon, so difficult to localize at the zenith, that I remain suspicious of the reality of this skittering reflection, a phenomenon which offers itself to only one sense and so vaguely that that sense cannot find sufficient support in it to call forth the perception of the whole body. When, on the other hand, a thing offers sufficient resistance to demand configuration, the entire phenomenal body, actual and possible, will contribute to that perception; I virtually see the tumbler I am holding in my hand, even though I am looking away.

The substantiality of the thing—its unity—is to be explained in no other way. This solves the dilemmas presented by the classical notions of substance. "The unity of the thing beyond its frozen properties is not a substrate, an empty X, a subject of inherence, but *that unique accent* which is rediscoverable in each [property], that unique manner of existing of which each property [considered by itself] is only a derived expression" (*PP,* p. 368). The fragility, rigidity, transparence, and crystalline sound of a tumbler translate a single way of being. Each quality invokes and unifies with the others because it is one of many holds the same perceiving body has on a moment of the world. For similar reasons, it is impossible to imagine a thing which is not either actually perceived or potentially perceptible. "The thing can never be separated from someone who perceives it, it can never be effectively en soi because its articulations are those of our existence and because it is posed at the term of a gaze or a sensorial exploration which bestows upon it a humanity" (*PP,* p. 370). Not surprisingly, Merleau-Ponty is here able to exploit to the full, though very much in passing, the advantages of the Berkeleian position that perception as such explains why our world is so "human." As we shall see later, however, he is also confronted with the Berkeleian problem of accounting for whatever objectivity, otherness, or en soi reality the perceived thing does obviously manifest.[27]

27. I have sought elsewhere to bring out the extent to which Berkeley anticipates this central development of transcendental philosophy. See "Berkeley," in Etienne Gilson and Thomas Langan, *Modern Philosophy* (New York, Random House, 1962).

"The whole of nature is the staging [*mise en scène*] of our own life or our interlocutor in a sort of dialogue" (*PP*, p. 370). The poetic language in which this declaration is couched (invoking theater and discourse) itself brings home strikingly the advantages of this aesthetic philosophy. If the thing is indeed the correlate of my body, if it is the corps propre which provides the very texture of the world, then, to begin with, the existence of anthropomorphic predicates is explained once and for all in a truly international sense. The "gay colors," for example, are now gay "out there" in the world, as real qualities of things themselves. This explains why the world, instead of seeming normally a hostile, foreign reality, presents itself first of all as so many projects for our praxis. It is a home, an intersubjective society, *accueillante* and viable, and only in rare moments can raw being be sensed as the ultimate indifference of the nature which has thrown up on its shores this *cariatide du vide* whose intentionality manages to carve out for itself a livable milieu. The obvious truth that our projects can insert themselves in the world while, at the same time, the world can motivate those projects no longer poses the least problem for the phenomenological philosopher.

Merleau-Ponty also masterfully capitalizes on the Berkeleian aspects of his position to explain the role of the implicit, the negative —the shadow as well as the light all those "unities of value" that unquestionably enter into the lived constitution of our experimental fields and confuse the rationalist approach. Perception grasps, in the words of Max Scheler, not just the explicitly posed, "but everything whose existence *or inexistence,* whose nature *or alteration* count *practically* for me."[28] If someone has taken a painting out of a room I know well, I can perceive that there has been a change without

28. Max Scheler, *Der Formalismus in der Ethik und die materiale Wert-ethik,* p. 140, cited *PP,* p. 371. That a phenomenology oriented toward a theory of truth as praxis should have been influenced by Scheler is of course not surprising. Indeed, it is no exaggeration to say that Merleau-Ponty's whole enterprise is a prolongation of the tradition advanced by Scheler of a phe-nomenology parallel to Husserl's and studiously avoiding his intellectualism. Unfortunately, however, Merleau-Ponty does not seem to have been struck by Scheler's criticism of the limits of praxis. Cf. the chapter on Scheler in Gilson, Langan, and Maurer, *Recent Philosophy.*

knowing precisely what has occurred. Similar examples are the keyed-up feeling produced by a gathering storm, the express signs of which I cannot enumerate, the elements of peripheral vision that the hysterical person does not grasp expressly but that nevertheless co-determine his movements and orientation, or the faithful friendship to which I hardly paid any attention but which must have existed for me, since its withdrawal leaves me somewhat uneasy.

Even after the pour nous in the formula for truth has been most adequately accounted for, the central problem remains the en soi—the transcendence, the otherness of the reality that perception grasps. Here Merleau-Ponty relies on the notion of field. The otherness of an experience which has just been said to be so human because it is mine is assured by its insurpassable plenitude. Every configuration, every comprehensible moment is supported by a generalized fond that fills the horizons with sense and seems always to do so no matter how they are extended, so that one implicitly presumes that, were one able to enclose it all as a totality, this totality would make sense. This parti-pris en faveur de l'être[29] which is founded with the corps propre is implicitly put to a test every time I form a project on the basis of a momentary configuration, but it is never put to the supreme test. Indeed, it never can be. Pourtant il y a quelque chose et non pas rien (PP, p. 381). I must always take up the sense that is offered me and, through the reprise of my project, practically extend it, but this determination is achieved without having to fulfill Leibniz's conditions for rationality.[30] Il y a du déterminé, au moins dans un certain degré de relativité. This we know by experience: That determination is lived directly as unity of style both of our existence as it unfolds to itself and of the things of our experience as they manifest themselves. Both types of unity of style are discovered against the background of the ultimate, the enduring, the experience of the world itself, the ground of all Being. The unity of the world is not grasped as Idea, for the new transcendental aesthetic does not look to the transcendental analytic for its ultimate principle. Rather, the

29. That "être" for Merleau-Ponty assumes the Parmenidean absoluteness of the idealist tradition is here patent.

30. These are outlined in "Leibniz," in Gilson and Langan, Modern Philosophy, p. 146.

transcendental unity of apperception, now unequivocally grounded in the corporeal synthesis, is given with the first perception as the field of all fields, the horizon of the unique world experience, the *omnitudo realitatis;* and it will continue until death, underlying all subsequent perceptions and serving as ground of their presumed ability eventually to refer to and unite themselves with all other perceptions as moments of a single reality (*PP,* p. 380). My knowledge of individual things always remains open, and over a long period of time I may perceive that the style of a person or the style of a town has changed. But "the world remains the same world throughout my whole life precisely because it is the permanent being interior to which I carry out all the corrections of knowledge, which corrections do not touch it in its unity, and whose evidence polarizes my movement toward the truth across all appearances and error (*PP,* p. 378).

Merleau-Ponty recognizes as clearly as the rationalists the need to provide an explanation for the ground of Being's unity, but he rejects the commonsense presumption that what is most fundamental must possess the kind of clarity and empty unity of the logically constructed idea. He affirms that reality manifests itself in the opaque unity of a horizon that is spilling over with richness and not in the geometer's idea, which is clear because it has been carefully constructed and is virtually empty. The world-unity that he describes as ground of substance-unity is synthetic and intentional without being rational and transparent. In the *Second Meditation* Descartes declared that the unity of the substance lay in an "intuition of the mind," a clear and distinct idea that could serve as a principle of unity for the qualities of the thing, which, though clear, could never be distinct. As the *Meditations* unfold, it soon becomes evident that the same principle provides both the unity of particular substances and that of the whole world, but it is never made very manifest exactly how the clear and distinct idea unifies. One cannot escape the impression that it is superior, not because it brings together and preserves in unity the various aspects of the material thing, but rather because it reflectively discovers its superiority to consist in its not needing the confused ideas in order to exist itself. In fact, the subject seems best off without those ideas in the holy reign of its own self-possessing unity. Now if the rationalist prejudice is reversed and we begin to rejoice with Merleau-Ponty in the "insurpassable plenitude" of the "resolutely silent Other," then a new principle of unity must be sought. This principle must respect the irreducible otherness revealed by the moments and, at the same time, keep the horizons of experience always open for the further revelations of that matter which alone legitimately motivates our intentions.

Merleau-Ponty clearly rejects the intellectualist conception of the cogito as an absolute self-possession and of Being as an Idea; for him, the Ego is the always partial conquest of a reflective self-grasp in the midst of an essentially dynamic, unsurpassably full, temporal experience in which every configuration is due to a separate perceptive act carried out against a background of world whose being—whose unity and consistency—is always only presumptive. This position obliges Merleau-Ponty to install at the very center of his ontology the principle of ambiguity: every configuration is a retensive-protensive gathering up of a structure from out of the flux of natural time. The anticipations of such structuring always exceed what is explicitly given (thus the perceptive object always has unplumbed horizons), and subsequent events can tend either to confirm or to weaken the initial engagement. I see a stone lying in my path, but when I come closer, I recognize it as a bright patch of sunlight. The "truer" second perception "corrects" the illusion because a richer hold on the givens has awakened the filling action of the entire corps propre more adequately. The sense of the data has become fuller because I have drawn into better range, because all my senses have been called into play, because I have been better motivated to attend. My initial perception must have presumed the presence of more data than was at any moment sensibly given. All perceptions do presume this, of course, for, according to Merleau-Ponty, what is sensibly given is never in itself as unequivocally and fully determined as the perceived thing built on the present data through the spontaneous contributions of the corps propre. Strictly speaking, every perception of its very nature can and will eventually stand corrected; we inevitably come to see the same matters not only more fully but also somewhat differently (*PP,* p. 396).

Thus, as was demonstrated in our earlier consideration of the experiences of night and dreams, the anticipatory structures of the corps propre are always actively reaching out, but in normal perception they encounter resistances, solicitations, points of data which call upon and can cooperate with all the active powers of the natural-sensing body and all the sedimentations of the cultural body to become configurated as meaningfully as the perceiver can make them. It is this harmony with past configurating, this full appeal to the several bodily powers, all of them capable of dealing meaningfully with this challenge, combined with its unexpectedness, its original indetermination, which give normal perception its substantiality—the impression it gives of being "out there" for everyone, of turning facets in all directions, not just that of the perceiver.

The hallucination—whose existence this philosophy has the immense merit of being able to account for convincingly—is singularly instructive precisely because of its contrast to normal perception. The hallucination does enjoy at least a meager sort of intentionality; the sick person believes in his hallucinations because his body, then as always, is devoted to bringing a world into being. But, very significantly, he cannot believe in them in exactly the same way that healthy individuals do, for the simple reason that they do not enjoy the full-fleshed reality of normal perception. Psychologists have established this by first carefully eliciting the fullest possible description of a hallucination and then installing a real object where the hallucinatory one was supposed to have appeared. When, for example, a patient who said, "When I wake up in the morning, there is a green snake, so big, coiled there on the rug," saw a real snake there, he manifested a fright with which the imaginary snake had never been honored. When a patient who complained of hearing voices heard the voice of a doctor projected from behind a screen, he declared, "This time, it's a *real* voice." The corollary also stands: the hallucination lacks the real world's intersubjective character, as the sick person often realizes when he asks a question such as, "Don't you hear my voices?"[31] and then goes on to say, "I'm the only one who hears them." Hallucinations play themselves out on a stage different from that of the perceived world. "Look," declares a sick person, "while we're talking, somebody says this, then somebody says that, and

31. In Minkowski, *Le Problème des hallucinations et le problème de l'espace,* p. 64, cited *PP,* p. 390.

where could all that come from?" The hallucination does not seem tied to everything else, disregards the consistencies of normal time and space, lacks that internal articulation of various equivalent properties which makes the true thing rest en soi; it is not "stuffed with little perceptions," as Leibniz would say, that support it in the real world. Most hallucinations have but one facet; they are ephemeral phenomena—pinpricks, shakings, breaths of air, chills, sparks, brilliant points, silhouettes—and when a real thing is involved in them, it is represented only by its bare style or physiognomy. The sick person's rapport with real things is always one of coexistence rather than cooperation. He is incapable of distinguishing the patterned from the fortuitous; the consciousness of the fortuitous presupposes the grasp of precise and distinct causal series. He lives alone in the disconnected debris of a world. He seizes, among the debris, whatever active montage suits his purposes and utilizes it without consistent reference to everything else to flesh out his private sick intentions; he thus fabricates a false personal world out of the real world's ruins (*PP*, p. 393).

Merleau-Ponty leaves no doubt about the far-reaching implications of such ambiguous phenomena. "The hallucinatory imposture will never be understood unless apodictic certitude is taken away from sensation and full self-possession from perceptive consciousness. The existence of the perceived is never necessary, as the perception presumes an explicitation which would go to infinity, and which, for that matter, could gain on one side only by losing on the other and would have to expose itself to the risk of time." Only in *presumption* —that is, in the anticipatory fixing-projections of objective thought —is there any final solution. Presumption alone can establish not only the thing but also the abstract Ego, since my concrete self is really intentional and presumptive (*PP*, pp. 396–97). The limits and legitimacy of the presumptions of objectifying reason will be discussed in the next chapter. But the new transcendental aesthetic already leaves no doubt that in itself the reality encountered in space and time by a perception founded in the finite body's ambiguity is and will ever remain *un mystère absolu*. Its discovery will never be complete. The problem of truth itself is thus not a problem after all but a mystery. There is an eternal contradiction in the very notion of a finite truth, of a consciousness attaining to a real other in time. Merleau-Ponty has rejoined, through the Logic of Hegel, Book Lambda of Aristotle's *Metaphysics*—Hegel has now really been "turned upside down."

The philosophy of Being is phenomenology because the insertion through the body into the world is ambiguous, because *l'être au monde* means not only to be in the world, but to belong to a world which transcends any individual. Phenomenology does not set out to explain by reducing the many moments of an experience to the stable, clear and distinct structure of an idea. Rather, it seeks to describe, using intellectual (and therefore fixed) instruments to direct attention toward a reality that is essentially dynamic and open (i.e. toward the fond and the horizons that surround and support every temporary configuration and tie it to the living whole of the historical discourse). I am "in and of the world" through my body; thus my perception reveals an object whose transcendence keeps it from being mine: instead of belonging to that unique point of ego which is the consciousness' grasp of itself, it escapes my comprehension in every direction; it drags in with itself unexpected structures and horizons unfamiliar to me; it challenges me to conquests I never knew were in me. In a very real sense, it is not I who perceive: *on perçoit en moi.* This very generality of my perception moves my gaze toward those others who are implicated in it from their own points of view in time and space, revealing a central aspect of the mystery of our existence in the world, its intersubjectivity. This discovery is the climax of Merleau-Ponty's transcendental aesthetic.

THE COEXISTENCE OF EGOS IN AN INTERSUBJECTIVE WORLD

Merleau-Ponty's exploitation of the notion of a corporeally grounded generality as fond of every perceptual act so successfully eliminates the problem of intersubjectivity that, instead of finding himself faced with the difficulties confronting Husserl in the Fifth *Cartesian Meditation,* he has to take pains to show how in such a world the problem of solipsism could ever arise.

That solipsism is in fact a problem that genetically arises only in later stages of development has been established in psychological studies of the very small child. He lives as exclusively as humanly possible in a world which he believes to be totally accessible to all those about him. With no self-awareness, the child does not suspect that he is—as, in fact, are all of us—restricted to a point of view. He never submits his thoughts to criticism but simply accepts them as they arise, without seeking to introduce stronger connections between them than they spontaneously offer. People are for the child empty heads attached to a single evident world where everything takes place—even dreams, which he thinks are "in the room." Even thought, for him, is "in the world," because he makes no distinction between thought itself and the words which express it.[32] It is when a child does begin to develop self-awareness and when, at about the age of twelve, he begins to achieve a veritable cogito and rejoins the truths of rationalism, that the battle of consciousnesses Hegel's *Phenomenology* has described begins. For that battle to take place, the consciousness that I am must suspect the presence of foreign consciousnesses. The child's ingenuous being-in-the-world remains below the level of cogito as a necessary part of its constitution, as its avenue into the intersubjective world.[33]

To encounter a foreign comportment is not simply to encounter another thing but rather a kind of attentional field of attraction into which my world seems sucked, so that our two bodies form a single system in a common world, like the two sides of a coin. Merleau-Ponty illustrates this point by such phenomena as the fact that a little baby opens his mouth when one takes his finger into one's mouth as though one were going to bite it. Such facts are best explained by the anonymity-generality implicit in the notions of a common field. "There is one single phenomenon, and the anonymous existence of which my body is the trace at every moment after the initial encounter inhabits both bodies simultaneously."

32. Merleau-Ponty cites Piaget, as we might expect. It is worth remembering that Merleau-Ponty early in his academic career specialized somewhat in child psychology. One of his most interesting courses is available from the Centre de Documentation Universitaire under the title "Les relations avec autrui chez l'enfant."

33. "The barbarous thoughts of the first age remain as an indispensable *acquis* down under those of the adult age." *PP*, p. 408.

Another person's perspectives and mine are not mutually exclusive but—like the profiles that fit together to form a single thing—slide (*glissent*) into one another (*PP*, p. 406). The earlier explanation of how *Abschattungen* slide together to form a constant thing (see p. 54) is thus effortlessly extended to the problem of intersubjectivity. The corps propre's generality provides the unifying fond whose horizons encompass the two Abschattungen. By its very nature, that generality includes a multiplicity of points of view onto the same experience; it essentially transcends the explicit self-aware Ego, which discovers itself only within its horizons, for it establishes that Ego's prehistory, given it at birth, destined to be taken away at death, and thus seals the Ego within the horizons of its transcendence. Having thus, in a sense, absolute precedence over me, transcending in its givenness every moment of experience so that experience itself is seen to be always part of a reality already "out there," the corps propre, due to its generality, is essentially able to interlace naturally with other Egos caught up in its general structure. The full force of the declaration that we are *au monde* can now be appreciated. We belong to the world more than the world belongs to us; it is always already there for us, proposing its projects to us, taking our projects back into itself, and grounding the very possibility of Egos.

Nevertheless these Egos do exist. The problem of solipsism has been raised throughout the history of philosophy, and the hostile stare of the Other confronts us as an unpleasant fact. Even the smoothest mutual undertakings originate in the projects of separate individuals, each operating from the depths of his own subjectivity. Merleau-Ponty even feels justified in declaring, "It would be hypocrisy to believe that I wish the good of the Other *as my own,* since even that attachment to the good of the Other still comes from me" (*PP*, pp. 409–10). Though I am transcended on every side by my own acts and virtually drowned in their generality, I am nevertheless the ego through whom they are all lived. The very fact that every affirmation, every engagement, every doubt, even every negation takes place in a field opened before the individual act itself suffices to point out the irreducible importance of the self. It is actually supported by the generality which founds for it the natural and cultural world, but it must be recognized as "an insatiable being who appropriates all that it can encounter, to whom nothing is ever purely and simply given, because he has received the world as his lot (*en partage*) and therefore carries in himself the project of all possible beings, because he has once and for all been sealed into his field of experience" (*PP*, p. 411). The invocation of the anonymous generality of the body does not really by itself adequately explain how the indeclinable I can alienate himself for the sake of the other, since it is exactly offset by the other dimension of generality, that of my inalienable subjectivity. It was, after all, the fact that it is I who am always conscious that initially gave rise to constitutive idealisms.

Merleau-Ponty's answer to this paradox is summed up in a single formula, the proper understanding of which introduces us to his theory of liberty: "I am given to myself." To affirm that I am given is to state that the consciousness discovers itself already in the world, depends on the world for its motives, and is incapable of surviving the world. Merleau-Ponty speaks of this absolute dependence on what is Other as a *savor of mortality*. The historical necessity structured by my reprise of the worldly event is a necessity dependent on the contingent fact that I am the kind of comportment I happen to be; that is why the world presents itself to me as it does. This dependency of the Ego on what precedes and surrounds its act for the very material of the intention affirms that it is of the Ego's very essence to be turned toward that which is other than it.

But I am given to myself; I am not absolutely bound to any one of the intentions that the world proposes. The self retains a *faculté de recul* (*PP*, p. 413)—a capacity for backing up—for the personal dimension of the corps propre's generality arms me with the existential space-opening ability that permits a domination of the field, which (as *Phenomenology* and *Signs* both declare) is the very possibility of thinking. But this ability to command the field's structure by commanding the ways in which the horizons open toward the future is the antithesis of Absolute Ego's unmotivated constitution, and Merleau-Ponty offers for its limits a superb formula that clearly emphasizes both the "I am given" and the "to myself": "I can only get away from being by fleeing into being" (*Je ne puis fuir l'être que dans l'être*). "I flee from society into nature or from the real world into the imaginary which is made of the debris of the real" (*PP*,

p. 413). Another formula—which we noted earlier and the implications of which we shall consider later—comes to mind: I am not a *trou dans l'être*—that is, not a hole, groundless *néant*—but a *creux* or a *pli*, a fold in Being which is formed by Being's turning back on itself, reflecting. These suggestions can be exploited when, later, we seek to understand Merleau-Ponty's conception of a finite liberty, of a real initiative that is never an absolute initiative. In the opening of the time-space necessary for existence, Being is not opposed by Nothing; rather, the proper function of the human comportment is to be able, so to speak, to play off a part of Being against other parts. As capacity to create a space within Being, our freedom is nothing but a certain initiative in determining the structure of a phenomenal field, in seizing a point of view on the whole.

This initiative finds its most human, we might say its most personal, expression as thought, and it is evident that before making a final effort to understand the implications of the extraordinary description of finite liberty toward which *The Phenomenology of Perception* is ordered, we must consider this objectivizing, time-conquering activity first in its own right. The limits of its pretensions will prove particularly interesting for the light they cast on the very conditions of our existence.

CHAPTER 3

Analytica-Dialectica

As We Have Seen, Merleau-Ponty succeeded in sketching out a transcendental aesthetic that, far from depending on the synthesizing of a self-possessed Cogito, grounds the possibility of reflection in the prereflexive existence of perception. This success enabled him to launch a final critique of any form of the Cogito which, like the Cartesian, would pretend to be *pensée pure*. The main points of his critique can by now be grasped in even a brief summary.

(1) The Cogito, far from being an immediate self-possession, comes to know itself only in and through its acts of knowing the world: *Je suis à moi en étant au monde* (PP, p. 466).

(2) Since it is tied to its progressive unfolding of a perceptive grasp on the world, the Cogito's self-possession can never be total; it is not that of a pensée pure but of an existential style which only gradually takes possession of itself as it unfolds in time. Hence, *J'ai bien des choses à apprendre sur moi-même* (PP, p. 436).

(3) As the Cogito is not a pensée pure but is rather a point of view in the world, no pure act of thinking can achieve absolute clarity—that is, complete and unalterable unity of the world or even of any one of the things in the world. Such unity as can be achieved is always lived and is inevitably presumptive.

(4) But our understanding does pretend to a kind of necessity and totality for its ideas. Therefore, when seeking to show that *la pensée formelle vit de la pensée intuitive* (PP, p. 441), Merleau-Ponty is obliged to carry his critique not only beyond Kant—the temporalization of the Idea being here as thoroughgoing as in Hegel—but also beyond Hegel. His existentialization of necessity is radical and allows

no structure of movement whatever to enjoy metaphysical precedence over the moments of its own development. In this sense, Merleau-Ponty's critique is as thorough as Marx's, to which it obviously owes much; but it manages to avoid the naïvetés of Engels' scientism by grasping the ultimate implications of its own aesthetic starting point.

Nothing in the tradition of transcendental philosophy can compare with the poetics in which Merleau-Ponty's analysis so naturally and inevitably culminates. Unfortunately, however, his actual critique of the pretension of ideas to achieve "clarity" is not very extensive either in the *Phenomenology* or later in *Signs*. As he hurries on to deepen the positive implications of his own position, he is content simply to indicate how a few extreme examples of idealization in fact do not transcend the limits of *la pensée intuitive,* upon which they ultimately depend. This haste hides a weakness that we shall eventually seek to point out.

(5) The positive corollary of this critique is the notion of *cogito parlant;* the ultimate reality has been transferred from the thinking Ego (Cogito) to the Ego-in-the-world which takes possession of itself and of things through expressive acts. If the being of things and my own existence manifest themselves as *sens,* then expression, which is the act of taking up and extending a sens, is obviously the central phenomenon in human life. The culmination of this analysis offers insight into why the subjectivity, though indeclinable, and thus a kind of absolute, is at the same time dependent—is a relative absolute. I am the constituent of my thought in general (to say otherwise would be to suppose there is a truth without anyone to know it), yet I do not command absolutely any one thought (every one always escapes my total grasp, and none totally occupies the field of my consideration), which is why I can always withdraw into that depth of non-being from out of which the subjectivity surges (*PP,* p. 459). The paradox of a perceptually grounded truth here receives its most significant formulation.

JE SUIS DONC JE PENSE

Though Descartes is the ostensible foil of this onslaught, it is meant in reality to make every traditional philosophy cringe. Husserl and Sartre are most obviously *en vue* for having made of the pour soi a principle too self-possessed. Kant himself is under fire to the extent that he failed to make it clear enough that the deduction of the categories is a revelation of an understanding grounded in a corporeal existence, for whom time and space are not simply structures to be superimposed on a sensible matter but the very way the body lives its experience.[1]

It should be clear from the outset that, in criticizing the pretensions of the Cogito, Merleau-Ponty is not calling into doubt any aspect of its reality—not even its ability to withdraw from the world which founds it, to doubt that without which it could never be in the first place. He is not trying to wish away the thorny aspects of the Cogito's existence. But he is obliged and willing to reinterpret those aspects in order to establish the exact conditions of free withdrawal.

I *can* doubt—so much is true—but only if I am already thinking, and thinking about things known in the world. Hence the illusory nature of Descartes' notion of a *pensée de voir*—the idea that I can doubt that which I see but cannot doubt the thought, "I am seeing"; in other words, that the sensation in itself cannot be erroneous but only our interpretation of it. Why should the knowledge that I see be more immediate than the knowledge that I see this thing? Since to see is always to see something, I must have seen something first in order even to know now that I am seeing. Moreover, the interpretation of whatever it is that I see is always motivated by the very structure of the sensations themselves. In other words, the certitude of an exterior thing is enveloped in the very manner in which the sensation articulates itself and develops itself before me. This red, for instance, may be either opaque red on a single plane or a reddish atmosphere with three dimensions. The judgment surges up from this sensual ground. Hence there is no sphere of immanence, no domain where consciousness is strictly *chez elle* and assured against all risk of error (*PP,* p. 431). Since consciousness is nothing but active transcendence,

1. Kant is closest to Merleau-Ponty in the passages in which he shows the inherent temporality of the *Begriffe* of the understanding; Heidegger has interpreted the existentialist passages of the *Kritik* in his *Kant and the Problem of Metaphysics,* trans. J. Churchill (Bloomington, Indiana University Press, 1962). See also Paul Ricoeur's article, "Kant et Husserl" in *Kantstudien,* 46 (1954), 44–57.

sensations cannot be passively noted as psychic events closed in upon themselves and leaving uncertainties about the reality of the things seen.

If it now begins to seem rather wondrous that I can doubt at all, it becomes even more so after Merleau-Ponty has finished the next stage in his attack. There he turns to what is surely the favorite haunt of subjectivism—the affections—and succeeds in showing that, far from being turned in on themselves, even they transcend. He points out that it does make sense to talk, as we commonly do, of a true and a false love. Even though when I am in the throes of a false love I do not know that it is false, I can later come to recognize it to have been so. When only a part of me loves an accidental part of another—as when the middle-agedness of a man responds to the freshness and vitality of a young girl—the reality of that incompleteness does not appear to me, since, were that the case, I would know that this is not love. But when the spell is broken—when, precisely, I do become aware of what it was that bound me—I can recognize that the other aspects, and thus the real unity of the situation, were always surging unnoticed below the appearances I had chosen to structure. As long as I can believe in the object I give myself, the error is momentarily absorbed into the scheme I am imposing on my life; it reveals itself only when the tension created between my ordering of the appearances and the ever-intruding reality allows elements that my scheme simply can no longer handle to erupt into consciousness. The situation finally reaches the point where my basic projections are so under attack by the data their field is intended to interpret that I become strongly motivated to bring the projections, and thus the field, into line with the later facts. I then break with the old course of things that just cannot go on any longer. From that moment, all the old events are seen in a very different light and the hypocrisy of acts which were seemingly carried out in absolutely good faith is recognized. Events revealing the superficiality of my engagement have proven that such acts were in fact truly hypocritical.

Even in its own most subjective realm, that of the affections, the Cogito does not attain pure, transparent self-possession, identity with itself. The main thrust is not just that at any one moment the ultimate sense of my acts is not revealed to me or that "I have a lot to learn about myself" (*PP*, p. 436); it is not even that the Cogito has no *chez lui,* no realm where it grasps something, if only just itself, utterly, totally, unequivocally, certainly. It is rather more positive: The Cogito exists in its acts, and these reveal it as engaged in a world. The Cogito's acts progressively achieve its active grasp of things and accomplish correlatively and progressively its realization and possession of itself as it expresses itself in the structuring of its world. A Cogito is present from the very beginning of any human experience, since everything that is happening is, after all, *my* experience, a "unique experience, inseparable from itself, a single 'cohesion of life' [Merleau-Ponty borrows the phrase *Zusammenhang des Lebens* from Heidegger], a single temporality which explicates itself from its birth on and confirms itself in each present moment" (*PP*, p. 466). The essential being of this Cogito is being-in-the-world, *In-der-Welt-sein,* and, therefore, temporality. Since it must operate from a point of view, it can never be absorbed totally by any one perception or rest in any one profile. It is destined to move out as a motricity to the encounter with the world. The key to understanding the kind of self-possession, of unity, that the finite perception-rooted Cogito actually lives—and, noematically, the ultimate sense of our pronouncements—lies in the study of the way in which the existent structures for himself a lived time.

The pretense of our ideas to pronounce eternally the truth of essences is the thorniest problem here, and Merleau-Ponty's notion of a finite, temporal Cogito demands nothing less than a new interpretation of the ground of rational necessity. In seeking to show that the understanding's "presumption of a truth for all times" is nothing but an extension of the perception's fixing of a thing—the encounter with a material essence which itself is a presumptive synthesis rooted in the very way the body opens for itself a space by means of temporal horizons—Merleau-Ponty lays the groundwork for his conception of a purely historical truth.

FORMAL THOUGHT LIVES OFF INTUITIVE THOUGHT

The idea of a triangle is one of those ideas which somehow seem to give us possession of the very essence of a reality that is not bound to a particular place and time. Such ideas seem to have a sort of sphere of their own, an eternity; the origin of this impression of necessity requires closer examination.

First of all, in what more exactly does the necessity of the triangle consist? When I am demonstrating a triangle, I refer to a certain relationship among lines drawn that binds me. The child can add a line to his drawing of a train and then declare it a house, but arbitrary addition to the triangle will make it cease to be a triangle, whatever I may say about it. Secondly, the triangle is a stable structure in that the relationship between the ensemble of givens that form the hypothesis and the conclusions I can draw from them survives the flow of time enough to make possible repeated demonstrations on an indefinite number of empirical figures. It is this fact that led the philosophers to imagine the existence of a time-transcending *eidos* and an Ego capable of a kind of absolute self-possession and able to intuit in the midst of a whole series of successive operations eternally valid conclusions (*PP*, p. 440).

The Phenomenology of Perception hardly denies that the experience of rationality does indeed involve some self-possession, some command of time, on the part of the Ego. But Merleau-Ponty insists that that temporality is fundamentally the body's perceptual being-in-the-world. As we said a moment ago, the stability of the idea is none other than that enjoyed by the perceived thing, and the fixing of the perceived thing is the very act of the body's existentially opening a space (*PP*, p. 445). "The perceptive synthesis," declares the *Phenomenology*, "is a temporal synthesis. The subjectivity on the level of perception is nothing other than temporality" (p. 276). Now if it is true that the "perceived thing's founding in us forever the ideal of [a] being which is what it is" is what makes possible "the phenomenon of Being"; that without it, for instance, "mathematics would appear to us a pure creation," then it is in the corporeal synthesis' opening of such a time-space that we must seek the ground and limit of idealization. "Thought is nothing 'interior'; it does not exist outside the world or outside of words" (*PP*, p. 213). The idealization of the triangle is thus nothing but an extension of the possibilities spontaneously offered by *la pensée intuitive*—namely, perception itself.

If men can think and animals cannot, it is because men perceive differently than animals. As *The Structure of Behavior* carefully develops, man's perception opens a space that offers the possibility of that kind of command of time which is brought to fruition in the use of symbol. In a key text of the *Phenomenology* Merleau-Ponty describes more explicitly and sustainedly than anywhere else his conception of this perceptual structuring. The discussion follows the declaration just cited to the effect that the perceptive synthesis is a temporal synthesis.

> When I open my eyes to my table, my consciousness is choked with colors and confused reflections [*reflets*]; it is scarcely able to distinguish itself from what is offered to it as it spreads itself out through the body into the spectacle which is as yet spectacle of nothing. Suddenly I fix the table which is not yet there; I look into the distance although there is as yet no depth; and my body centers itself on a still virtual object and distributes its sensible surfaces in such a way as to make it present [*le rendre actuel*].[2] I can thus send to its place in the world the something that was touching me, because I can, by backing up into the future [*en reculant dans l'avenir*], send into the immediate past the world's first attack on my senses and orient myself toward the determined object as toward an immediate future. The act of looking [*regard*] is indivisibly prospective, since the object is at the term of my movement of fixation, and retrospective, since [that object] is going to present itself as anterior to its apparition, as the stimulus, motive or prime mover in the world process since the beginning. The spatial synthesis and the synthesis of the object are founded on this deployment of time. In each movement of fixation my body ties together a present, a past, and a future; it secretes a time, or, rather, it becomes the place of nature where for the first time the events, instead of pushing one another in being, project about the present a double horizon of past and future and receive a historical

2. That the resemblance of these lines to the early sentences of *Du côté de chez Swann* is not coincidental is explicitly admitted when Merleau-Ponty quotes Proust's passage at length in a parallel context, p. 211n.

orientation. There is here indeed invocation, but not experience of an eternal *naturant*. My body takes possession of time, making a past and a future exist for a present; it is not a thing, for it makes time instead of submitting to it. (*PP*, pp. 276–77)

First, notice that it is clear here that, as Merleau-Ponty puts it elsewhere, the "intentions start from the field": perceptual fixing is not the act of a constitutive Ego, but rather is motivated by the perceptual situation. Note further that the thing can be as it is only as the result of the perceiver's act; it is not a reality en soi, but here, for instance, a certain disposition of surfaces made possible by the corporeally grounded act of *recul* into the future. The very way the thing is there for the perceiver is strictly human, essentially dependent on the specific way the human comportment is able to *ménager* the present, past, and future. Upon this depend all our possibilities for doing what we can do within our experiential fields; our ability to create, to move freely, to communicate. The animal intelligence, declares *Signs*, is absorbed completely in producing, as in a kaleidoscope, ever new landscapes for action; but man can do more than simply replace one sense, one meaningful structure, with another. He is capable of "substituting equivalent senses, the new structure presenting itself as having been already present in the old, the old one subsisting in it, the past being now *understood*" (*S*, p. 102). Merleau-Ponty stresses the dynamics of perception: "Every act of fixation has to be renewed; otherwise, it falls into unconsciousness" (*PP*, p. 277). The perceptual object remains focused in my field only as long as I keep scanning it actively; "volubility is an essential property of looking." In short, each perception is a separate act, with its field structured by the particular movement of the body in which it is based, not unlike the animal's individual *paysage d'action*. It is that perceptual moment which makes possible the fixing of the thing, but man demands that each moment's structural sense should reach beyond the narrowest dialectic of a minimal possible *paysage d'action* and find a kind of absolute truth by harmonizing with his global perception of the world with the totality of experience potentially present as fond of every discrete perception. Thus, any one human perceptual moment (with the exception of the very first, where there is only the prehistory of the brute corporeal synthesis) is able to ground further formalization precisely because previous acts of winning a permanent sense in perception are available here and now in every one of the things they already structured.

Merleau-Ponty can thus declare that the possibilities of further, consistent demonstration are not based on an analysis of an intuited *eidos* triangle "which contains to start with all that we are in due course able to draw out of it," but are based in the power of perception—"I effect the synthesis of the new property by means of the body which inserts me at one fell swoop in spatiality as a whole (*d'un seul coup dans l'espace*) and whose autonomous movement permits me to rejoin, through a series of precise steps, that global view of space" (*PP*, p. 444). The triangle incarnated in a physical thing, the triangle being perceived and not the triangle as *eidos,* is always ground of the formalizations, for the sense that I am able, by precise steps, to make explicit is latent from the first in that perceptual act. The intersubjective validity of my conclusions originates in the intersubjectivity of the perception of space, that always open, general, anonymous mode characteristic of the body. This conception by its very nature excludes the possibility that I—the expliciting Ego— should be considered as a self-transparent, self-commanding, absolutely creative, and willful giver of that sense. To prolong a side, to bring a parallel from a summit to the opposite side, or to put into play the theorem concerning parallels and their secants, I have to consider the triangle itself drawn on paper or presented in the imagination; I must consult its physiognomy, the concrete arrangement of its lines, its gestalt. I must return to the original spatial configuration I was given by my body. A logical definition of the triangle that will equal in fecundity the vision of the figure cannot be constructed. Even if I eventually build into my definition all the steps in the series of formal operations by which I have arrived at my present knowledge of it, they would still have had first to be discovered.

The fact that a formalization is always retrospective proves that it is never complete except in appearance—a conclusion of considerable critical significance. Appearance is of course very important, for there would never be any experience of truth and nothing would stop the volubility of our spirit if certain formal relations did not offer themselves as crystallized in particular things. We would not even be able to fix a hypothesis in order to deduce consequences from it if we did not start by holding it to be true. All the parts of the demonstration refer to the configuration of the triangle—to the way in which it occupies space, to the relations expressed by the words "prolong," "summit," "by," "on," etc. Now if such words have any sense, it is because I deal with the sensible or imaginary triangle situated at least virtually in my perceptual field, oriented with respect to up and down, right and left—that is to say, implicated in my general hold on the world. "The construction makes explicit the possibilities of the triangle considered, not according to the definition and as idea, but according to its configuration and as pole of my movements" (*PP*, p. 442). Only because the triangle is a structure held before me that presents itself first as an intention, an invitation to action offered by the world, do notions of "angle" and "line" really have a sense. And if I can attach one such structure (such as that of the triangle) to another (for instance, that of the parallels and secants), it is precisely because the first structure presents itself, not as fixed and dead, but as anchored in my living present and thus shot through with possibilities, with lines of force; from every part of it germinate directions not yet traced but possible (*PP*, p. 443). To the extent the triangle was offered as intention by the world, it was swelling with as yet undefined possibilities of which the demonstration I have just achieved is only one particular case.

That formalization, that explanation, that explication is never complete (*PP*, p. 441). Each act presupposes the presentation of the perceptual thing in a field, depends for its truth on the general sense that is latently structured into this given field, and gives it its past-future dimensions. In the first perception, this is contributed by the natural body alone; it is, as we said above, only a prehistory (an a priori like that which Paul Ricoeur describes as a *savoir-faire pré-formé*[3]) that permits the process to begin. For all other perceptions there is already operative a genuine cultural acquisition. As the body spontaneously installs me in a space, the accumulated sedimented general sense forms the horizons interior to which the attentive

---

3. Paul Ricoeur, *La Philosophie de la volonté,* Part I: "Le Volontaire et l'involontaire" (Paris, Aubier, 1949).

regard permits the thing to surge up. The making explicit itself
only actualizes a sense that was already latent as possibility prior to
the properly creative, sense-extending act of the actualizing regard.
The new sense causes us to understand what preceded, and the previous
grasp now appears to us obscure compared to the new crystallization
just achieved. Concurrently, this new point of view on the sense
of the past opens new possibilities for the future, as omitted old
possibilities crowd closer about the horizons, motivating further acts
of actualization, a clearer realization of what now appears to have
been present in the thing all along, though not very well understood.
Each new explicit act of making clear enriches the possibilities for
further exploitation, for new expressions—for further discourse on
the thing. This taking up of the offered sense into a new act of sense-
extending expression and the further reprise of the results of that
previous act into a still richer synthesis is the act that conquers time;
it founds history, and it provides the only eternity open to man. A
remarkable passage in the *Phenomenology* gathers all these considerations into a few dense sentences.

> Our body, to the extent that it moves itself—that is to say, to the
> extent that it is inseparable from a view of the world and that
> it is that very view realized—is the condition of the possibility
> not only of the geometric synthesis but, again, of all the expres-
> sive operations and all the acquisitions which constitute the
> cultural world. To say that thought is spontaneous does not
> mean that it coincides with itself but, rather, that it goes beyond
> itself (*se dépasse*); and the word is precisely the act by which
> it eternalizes itself in truth. (p. 445)

After this discovery, the problem of the possession of truth becomes
the problem of expression: (noetically) of the expressive act, and
(noematically) of language, art, and institutions as cultural facts or,
better, as cultural accomplishments. Only the analysis of these can
advance the endeavor to understand how the object is made present
to the subject, by rendering plausible the paradox of finite truth.
Merleau-Ponty's *analytica* becomes a *dialectica* in the sense that he
conceives pure ideas as existential, making of them historical acquisitions of culture, and the historicity of the dialectica is proved by

manifest indications that its principles are those of a praxis, which, we shall see, Merleau-Ponty conceives as the historical efforts of human society to realize itself evermore fully.

In seeking to understand Merleau-Ponty's conception of truth, our ultimate concern will be to understand his description of how there can be truths sufficient to polarize a common field of action for societies, truths that in some way prove fruitful. Merleau-Ponty's critical notion of truth is inextricable from his practical philosophy and his poetics. The *Phenomenology's* climactic theory of finite liberty, the political essays' stand on the ethics of history, and the aesthetic analysis in *Signs* are all keys to the philosopher's conception of the criteria and potentialities of truth. But for the moment we shall limit our consideration of the dialectica to its rather more negative critical task, that of challenging and reinterpreting the appearances that historically have given rise (noetically) to notions of the pure Ego and (noematically) to the notion of the eternally true idea made possible by the Ego's perfect self-possession.

EXPRESSION: THE COGITO'S SELF-DISCOVERY

The very existence of the concrete Ego is being-in-the-world; the only way a truly intentional Ego can be is to be acting—that is, by actually carrying out the task of structuring a field. Now the structuring of a field depends essentially on the horizons of world which provide the motives for the act and its continuity with all the other intentional acts that have been or can be—whether my own or those of other Egos. A brief consideration of the phenomenon of language will make the point most apparent.

When I wish to think a thought, I must express it either in internal discourse or by actually writing or speaking. To this end I draw on a linguistic treasury which presents itself as flexible possibilities, as intentions, as motivations; it is a stock of various ways of taking a stance, of moving about in a world of signification which functions as so many invitations to structure my intentional field in one way or another. Some of those possibilities I must espouse in order to incarnate—to give being to—my meaning. A writer must struggle to find words to express his exact meaning because, before

he actually manages to structure in the field of language a new signification, that meaning is only latent, like a vague tension, a dissatisfaction with the present structure or lack of structure, threatening it
from the horizons; only in expression does the new structuring of
the field bring the latent possibilities toward actualization. When
the writer "throws himself" into a sentence, it seems to move along
to completion according to a certain internal necessity; the words
well up spontaneously and bring with them the whole weight of
the sedimented sense as well as lines of forces leading to all the
unexplored corners of the horizons of language. Thus the writer
can discover more in what he has written than he was aware of
explicitly having intended, and the task of explicating its implications
will go on forever. "There is no analysis which can render language
clear and spread it out before us like an object" (PP, p. 448). Why
is this true? Why this strange independence of language, why this
ultimate obscurity? The previous description of the act of thinking
should remind us of the *Phenomenology's* description of the act of
vision and spatial orientation. We are born in the world of words
and language as we are born in the world of things and space. The
whole of it is given from the start, forever ripe for new restructuring
and new configurations. Every new configuration is but a rearrange-
ment of the field structured in the configurations of the past, hence
the unexpected coming-to-the-fore of points left on the horizons
by previous ones, hence the endless possibility of new configurations
taking off from the last one, permitting further discovery of other
points latent in the original field but left on the horizons by previous
configurations.

Even more than in the case of the perceptual fixing of the object,
fixing in language quickly reveals the extent to which the illusion of
stability, of a halt in the unending process of time-structuring expression, is indeed temporary and the possibility of making explicit with
perfect consistency presumptive. When I am actually speaking, I feel
quite certain about what is being said in such declarations as "I
waited a long time" or "Mr. Smith is dead." I am sure that I know what
I mean and that you understand me very well; but if I stop to wonder
about the nature of time or about the experience of death, there is
suddenly darkness all about (PP, p. 449). Nevertheless, I do manage

to speak (*Pourtant il y a quelque chose et non pas rien!*), just as I am able to move about in the space I do not comprehend. Acquisitions of meaning have been sedimented in the words which I find—by using them—accessible to me; they open a range of possible expression and invite me, in taking them up again, to extend creatively their sense, the direction and dimensions they sketched, in order to encompass a new meaning. Sense is already there in the words because previous acts of expression actually achieved the structuring of a field, because every reprise of earlier configurations in this field is an extension of them which actualizes new possibilities latent in that field following a given direction, a sense. Each act of linguistic expression is an event, creative in a limited, dependent way, a creation that depends on espousing the lines of force of what preceded, of a tradition. Each such happening opens a moment of time for all eternity; it will always be true to say that at this moment something took place, an act made possible by Being (that is, what is initially given as ground of all possibilities) and for which Being had been waiting forever. Sense, meaning, is nothing but this insertion in the web of Being's self-discovery. "Each moment of time, by its essence, poses an existence against which the other moments of time can do nothing" (*PP*, p. 450).

Here indeed is the ultimate necessity. Each moment of time, each acquisition of sense is sedimented and generalized, structuring the field of future possibilities by contributing the horizons in the form of possible linguistic motivations; "*each* present which is produced penetrates into time like an edge and pretends to eternity."[4] This is true even of an error—an expression whose inadequacy future

---

4. "We have, in traversing the past, only to do with what is *present;* for philosophy, as occupying itself with the true, has to do with the *eternally present.* Nothing in the past is lost for it, for the Idea is ever present; Spirit is immortal; with it there is no past, no future, but an essential *now.*" G. W. F. Hegel, *Philosophy of History*, trans. J. Sibree (New York, Dover, 1956), p. 79. Merleau-Ponty removes any suggestion that Spirit preexists its finite acts. Most Hegel interpreters agree that such was his position, too. See, for instance, the recent commentary of J. N. Findlay, *Hegel Re-Examined* (London, Allen and Unwin, 1958), p. 40. Hegel, too, according to the more recent commentators, sees Spirit operative in intentional acts that are yet far from achieving the self-possession and unity of acts of the Understanding.

perception will reveal. When I see this inadequacy, I rectify my opinion but it will forever be true that I arrived at the present truth via the
detour of that error, and hence the complexion of my present view
will not be quite the same as if I had never passed that way.

One aspect of this notion of necessity is especially important to
the task of the dialectica. Merleau-Ponty is here in effect pointing
out that the so-called eternity of the Ideal Truth is totally grounded
in the perceptive moment, which has as much necessity as the Idea.
To put it the other way around, the Idea has no more necessity than
the perception. "Eternity is not another order beyond time but is
the very atmosphere of time." The lasting truth of an idea (as we
shall see in the *Poetica*) results from its ability continually to absorb
present moments of experience because that which it expresses is
fundamental enough to remain relevant as dimension-structuring
horizons of explanation. Every truth of fact enjoys some of the necessity of a truth of reason because it is a part of our experience, because
it is inserted in the mesh of the corporeally grounded world. Thus
every moment of experience has some eternal necessity and remains
pertinent, like the Leibnizian monad, for every other moment; it is
true for all times. Conversely, every truth of reason—i.e. every expression which particularly strikes us by its claim to enduring significance—requires incarnation in moments of experience and must continue to be taken up in individual moments of experience (*PP*, p. 451);
Euclidian geometry came to be at a certain time because it was made
possible by a certain cultural preparation. Should the culture which
now supports it be destroyed, it would have to be reinvented. That
it could be reinvented while Beethoven's Ninth Symphony, if it were
forgotten by everyone and all scores were destroyed, could not is due
to the fact that the one expresses something that is closer to the
fundamental givens of the way our bodies are naturally in the world
than what the other expresses.

This radical historicization of the Idea itself serves the positive
purpose of rendering feasible a description of a finite liberty. It
illumines the fact that the Ego is never perfectly one with any of its
experiences, that the Cogito's unity is not the unity of the experience,
even though they found each other's very possibility, and hence that
the Cogito can hold itself apart from its experiences—can doubt.

This noncoincidence of the Cogito with the moment of experience leaves the existent free to overlook, to survey, and thus to influence the structure of the phenomenal field; this is the source of its ability to alter the world.

"Every fixing of an object, every apparition of a something presupposes a subject who ceases to interrogate himself at least in that particular connection (*PP,* p. 454). Even the positing of a hypothesis involves a certain halt in the flow of experience—a presumption, which, though motivated by what is happening within present phenomenal experience, nevertheless involves a certain "violence," the act of "backing-up into the future," which is that motivated anticipation itself. When I focus on something, I push everything else, including all other possible interrogations, to the margins of my experience because I presume that that upon which I am fixing my attention is more important. As I confine myself to my own act of fixing, trusting in the fecundity and significance of what is then going to appear, I exclude all else and, playing the game, let the invoked reality make its presentation; the cultural-perceptual synthesis then proceeds spontaneously, and I let it reveal what it will. "Only when I play the game, only when I engage myself, for instance, in a Euclidean space or a certain society, can the sense of that system begin to appear for me; only then can it become an *evidence."*

At no time do I have to play the game, however. I can withhold my commitment, and the motivations which are held out to me will not then receive the attention they are soliciting (much as in the case of illusion, when my anticipations are not filled up by the data I was expecting, but here reversed). But this withholding, this withdrawal from the potential evidences of a given field, is not the opposition of a *néant* to *l'être;* the Cogito is not a self-contained principle. Its very nature is to intend toward something; it is finite, sealed at birth into the world horizons. Consequently the withdrawal which its domination of the field permits is always a withdrawal from one moment of experience in favor of another. I can flee the social world by turning attention toward the natural, or I can flee the natural by turning to the imaginary, but even the imaginary reveals itself as world-relevant and world-grounded (*L'imaginaire est fait des débris du monde*). In every and any instance, the Cogito exists only in act

—that is, as corporeal act, as the movement of field-structuring carried out by a body espousing intentions in its world by taking up the movement they suggest and bringing them to a creative determination through anticipations. In a remark that can be extended to apply to the very possibility of freedom, "The relativity of movement is reduced to our power of changing *domaine* interior to the great world" (*PP*, p. 324).

When Merleau-Ponty writes in *Signs, La vérité est à faire,* he means not only that the corporeal-synthesizing of a sense is always a dynamic process—that even when a vector has been determined by an act of anticipatory fixing, this intention has to be kept from sedimenting by continual reprise—but also that this reprise itself is *à faire*—that the existent moves out to the encounter with the world by doing. It is only by engaging in action—whether it be the active *parcourant* of the sensible object by my regard, the demonstration of the properties of the triangle, engagement in a conversation, the creation of a work of art, or political action—that the sense of the phenomenon can be made to appear and a new series of possibilities for my engagement can present itself.

Thus it is that this phenomenological philosophy climaxes in a practica when it demonstrates that the discovery of ourselves is inseparable from the discovery of the world—not worldness in general, but the reality of the concrete world in which the human drama is actually being carried out. In the course of the next chapter we shall seek to show just how astonishingly concrete Merleau-Ponty's analysis is intended to be.

CHAPTER 4

Practica

THE PROBLEM OF FINITE FREEDOM

BY PROPERLY EXPLOITING the notion of being-in-the-world, under-stood as experience corporeally grounded in the activity of perception, Merleau-Ponty achieves in the last chapter of the *Phenomenology* one of his central contributions to philosophy: the old aporias of finite freedom are finally surpassed, in precisely the sense of Heidegger's notion of *Überwindung*. Although ultimately the ontology on which his argument rests does itself present classical difficulties in familiar form, the value of his doctrine of finite freedom should not be sacri-ficed. Whether it can be extricated from the insuperable problems of the aestheticism with which it is supported will be considered in our final chapter.

This new formulation seeks a *via media* between the old opposed errors of objectivism and subjectivism here represented, on the one hand, by the most radical form of Marxist materialism and, on the other, by Sartre at his nihilistic-voluntaristic extreme as "pure ra-tionalist" (*AD*, p. 158). The concrete significance—when applied to the political reality—of these positions for the present historical situa-tion will be considered later; here we shall sketch their general sense as theories of how the individual subject is related to the world in which he is situated.

The great merit of extreme Marxist materialism—and one which a successful description of finite liberty must emulate—is that it ac-cords the concrete reality of the situation a real weight (*HT*, p. 126). With its notion that the existent's acts are so real, so much "out there" in the world, as to be alienated from him, it presents the vision of a praxis that must be a genuine accomplishment in the objective order. In common experience, after all, freedom is always moving against a resistance, and acts leave indelible traces behind them. The problem with Marxism, however, is that objectivization there is so complete, the structures of the common socio-economic–political situation are conceived so much as a movement in matter, that it becomes difficult to explain with this philosophy how the individual can have any power over them. Indeed, it leaves one unclear how the Cogito could have any effective existence of its own beyond that of a vapid epiphenomenon, and even if it did, how it could insert its projects into that massive reality that is "out there." The self tends to become meaningless in the movement of materialistic determinism.

Sartre seeks to avoid these problems by placing the center of significance in the act of the existent, but he is then confronted with exactly the opposite difficulty, that of giving the generated history some weight. If it is this instant of initiative, my project, which determines the sense of the situation; if the past is only what I make of it now; if it is only the way I take up into my consideration the givens (the fact that I am a Jew or very rich) that gives them their sense (I am never reduced essentially to being myself a Jew or a rich man but am always centrally something above these facts); if a conversion suddenly changes the sense of a whole life—then it is difficult to see how we can explain the fact that the past does press on me; that it is improbable—an antirationalist category par excellence! (AD, pp. 158, 261)—if I have been raised in the most unenlightened bourgeois tradition, that I shall espouse the cause of the proletariat; that the facts impose limits on my projections; that feasible projects are distinguishable from foolish ones; and that, finally, my acts themselves bear lasting results, enduring beyond the moment of active will. Idealistic voluntarism erases not only the opposition of the others, but the reality of my very acts themselves and, in the process, the substance of my concrete self. Yet Sartre properly insists that I am ultimately *Sinngeber:* the improbable can happen; conversions do occur; my initiatives do reorder the significance of the facts; the resistances of the world are not absolute determinates; and the results of my acts are never irreversible.

Merleau-Ponty's reconciliation of the partial truths advanced by these opposed positions consists essentially of applying to the central problem the new phenomenological formulations intended to dissolve the basic subject-object aporia. Otherness must be conceived as placing real demands on the existent and resistances in his way without being *so* other as to be impermeable to his projects or *so* demanding as to render the notion of initiative totally inconceivable. Both extreme positions erroneously view the influence that the exterior can have on the self as causality, whether they accept or reject this notion.

To this notion of causality, Merleau-Ponty contrasts his own conception: motivation. The action of the Other on the individual center of initiative—on the Ego—is not like the deterministic, mechanical relationship upon which earlier physics relied. Such an unequivocal relationship is merely a conception, a product of objectivizing thought, not something primordially experienced. The points of resistance in my field of experience solicit—provoke, rather than form—my interpretation, calling forth a gamut of possible interpretative contexts according to which they will only then become more determined. It is in these terms, carefully prepared by the *Phenomenology*, that the manner in which I am motivated by my situation must be understood. As *être au monde*, I belong to the world in which I find myself situated; that is to say, at any moment of consciousness I discover myself as already given. I am already Jewish, rich, and bourgeois; I already exist in the world from a point of view, in middle-class society, in twentieth-century France; and I have been armed with certain prejudices, notions, and a language as set of possible expressions.

But these determinations are certainly not there in my world with the definiteness, the absolutely foreign otherness that characterizes things as conceived by unreflective common sense. "The dialectic inheres in a *field* of experience where each element opens on the other" (*AD,* p. 274). Even the resistance offered my projects by those of others does not have unequivocal, absolute otherness. As was the case with perception, I always confront any point of resistance or of impulse in my experience—be it a part of my sedimented history, advice expressed by another person, or whatever—from within the sense-giving horizons of my whole being-in-the-world. Since I belong to the world because it needs me to bring it to expressed existence, no given can be totally foreign to me. All solicitations or obstacles I may find within my world need this world to appear at all and must derive their sense ultimately from the capacity to structure which I bring to the perceptive act; they present themselves more as intentions, potential vectors, invitations to action, than as unequivocal objects or absolute determinations.

This is not to say, of course, that I am the source of the givens, or that I can make of them what I wish. Whatever sort of resistance or impulse may be operative—from here-and-now sensible givens, through intentions proposed expressly by other Egos, to the weight of my own generalized past—they are certainly not nothing. Indeed, such realities are clearly other than the central point of initiative, the Ego itself, which, as the locus of natural time, can never be alienated in any of its moments. The ambiguous motivational relationship I enjoy with the external world reflects the central paradox of existence founded in time: this Ego, which by its essence cannot be caught up in any Abschattung but founds the very possibility of any and all Abschattungen, is nevertheless also that which by essence can only find itself outside itself, in its reprise of an Other to which it must give sense in order to express itself—in order to be at all.

Hence Sartre's assertion that our freedom from all Others consists in our ability to deny and to withdraw is seriously misleading. Our capacity to deny an obstacle or a solicitation is nothing more than our ability to integrate it in a new sense-structure wherein it loses its relative intensity and may even be registered only as absent. The important aspect of our nature brought into play here was first discovered under the misleading form of the body-soul relationship and only recently rethought in terms of Husserl's notion of *Fundierung;* it is the peculiar relationship that exists between the higher levels of integration of a stratified organism and those lower moments upon which they depend. Merleau-Ponty's addition to this development is the discovery of the ability of the Ego to shift itself off center within this complex polarity. This maneuver never removes it from intentionality, but is rather a shift of attention—a change of interpretation—that can only occur because it is able to play one moment of reality off against another, to outweigh one solicitation with another, and then to balance and combine both in a constellation of new sense.

Thus I can withdraw, deny, doubt, solely by moving into a different world: "I can flee being only into being." When I turn resolutely away from politics, I must affirm some other value instead, such as the overriding importance of nature. This is similar to those moments when, because I wish not to be distracted by the buzzing confusion going on about me, I plunge myself into work capable of holding my attention or when, wishing to stop seeing black and white squares on the floor as a staircase pattern, I force them to organize themselves as stars or cubes.

This ambiguous but total motivating power of the world governs even the most personal decisions. Freud, who recognized the reality of our incarnation, saw this when he explained comportment as sexuality. He was seeking, not to lower the spirit, but to spiritualize the flesh; avoiding a mechanistic view of the soul, he saw the sense latent in our incarnation because he had discovered in the body "its symbolic and poetical charge."[1] When he describes the subconscious as latent Being waiting for more articulated realization, for expression in the individual personality ("*Wo Es war, soll Ich werden*"), when he explains mental difficulties, complexes, and fixations as failures, through lack of energy, to open properly to this subconscious sea, to tear new reality out of it, to structure it and give it a sense in a personality; when he visualizes man not as an immanent ready-made natural being—a machine among machines—but as the *chantier* where preconstituted being matures in movement, Freud is incontestably Merleau-Ponty's direct predecessor. My freedom is thus motivated from the "inside" and the "outside" at the same time, through my body—this secretion of my whole history, where nature and second nature have become indiscernible, which is the channel of all external opposition as well as the means through which I keep expressing and incarnating myself. Only as incarnated in such a *corps propre* can human freedom be understood at all. In describing perception as the foundation of comportment, Merleau-Ponty often emphasizes that movement is the spontaneous maturation as well as the mode of vision; as the French phrase, *le corps se meut,* suggests, the body moves itself, spontaneously, without needing conscious

1. Hesnard, *L'Œuvre de Freud* (Paris, Payot, 1960), p. 7.

direction from any soul or Ego discrete from it. This is true in the most personal aspects of existence. The body is this strange locus where the self experiences the world and where this experience spontaneously matures into comportments which make further experiences both possible and richer.

Sartre is correct in asserting that I can always convert (a radical change of course being a central possibility of my freedom) and that maturation must imply neither straightness of course nor dearth of surprises. But conversion is not achieved by pure fiat. I really am given to myself, having a past to which I also belong, in just the sense that I both possess and am possessed by my body. I cannot live outside the time and space of that past; every one of my acts animates and moves about its weight. I can succeed in changing radically the fundamental direction, the style of my whole life, only by espousing a real and powerful solicitation—itself also given—which will be able, when integrated, to turn aside the whole natural (in the sense of second nature) vector of my life up to that point. Thus the sup-plications of another or the gathering weight of particular percep-tions that are irreconcilable with certain ground convictions are of utmost importance; they help to sediment a counterforce that may bring the individual to the vision that ripens in the moment of decision. Even after conversion has occurred, the past does not dis-appear. It continues to guard that eternity which Jung has shown to be the prerogative of every moment of experience. The Marxist leader who is a converted bourgeois intellectual will never be the same Communist as he who has roots in the proletariat.

This approach deals a deathblow to the old subjectivist fascination for decision as moment of totally free, independent choice. Decisions do not take place in a vacuum. As all other human acts, they are expressions—that is, moments of initiative in the crystallization of a field of meaning. They are thus free, in that they decenter and recenter that field; but this freedom is very finite as they cannot be extricated from their matter—their givens—out of which they welled up, which they prolong, restructure, and illumine in new directions. In the course of a deliberation, every crystallizing act on my part tends to throw light on the matter which wells up from the corps propre to fill up my intentions (*AD*, p. 266). Expressions can no more be separated from their organ—the sedimented self that wills them—than a gesture can be separated from the body which makes it and that body's space.

It is not difficult to understand, then, why a lucid and honest man finds it so difficult to explain when exactly and how he made an important decision. My noisiest moments of deliberation, which often conceal my bad conscience about the fact that my decision has actually already been made, must never be mistaken for the real process of deciding which has been going on silently throughout my entire personal history as my acts sedimented and formed the future general horizons whose solicitations are calling today for this given act. This is not to say that the Ego is without influence on the present moment, however, as another comparison with the attentive act will make clear. If an explosion occurs outside my window while I am writing this, the probability is slight that I shall be able to resist turning my attention toward the noise, smoke, and flames; but this is an extreme case. Normally I can focus (though never perfectly) on whichever given I choose. Similarly, an outburst of unleashed passion which dredges up a long and sordid history of questionable acts from the depths of my second nature can also destroy the delicate equilibrium within which the initiatives of the free Ego can exercise a pivotal influence. Usually, however, I am free in both kinds of situations to influence creatively the structuring of a field of decision. This freedom is founded on the "insurpassable generality of the Ego," its capacity for transcending the moment of any one experience, for "backing up into the future," and for guiding the process of reprise. Because of this ability, I can balance consideration against consideration and reign over the structuring of the deliberation. It should be remembered, however, that my freedom is finite. The world also makes its demands as it confronts me with its genuine otherness, in which the truth or the light have already been incarnated.

THE HUMAN NATURE OF THE WORLD'S DEMANDS

That I am motivated by the "Not I" without being determined by a foreign reality becomes still more comprehensible when the humanized quality of the givens with which we have to contend is considered. Most fundamental, of course, is the principle of the corps propre's natural anonymity: not only is generality an essential mode of its intentionality (I am a man, i.e. my perception is grounded in a principle no more exclusively mine than an other's), but also, reciprocally, the constituted world I meet and know is the product of a synthesizing act of a body which I can, nonetheless, speak of as a piece of matter that is actually mine, the corner of reality interior to which I live. We can thus actually say of the world that "we carry its fundamental structures with us" (*PP*, p. 377).

If the world is already human in this fundamental, natural way, it is even more evidently so in its all-pervasive cultural reality. Most of the intentions which my act of reprise takes up are humanized ones. I reach things through symbols, especially through words, in which are gathered up the accumulated dealings of mankind; such symbols are natural nuclei about which sedimented intentions cluster. Most of the things I encounter are themselves molded by human intentions into cultural objects—cultivated fields, tools, passageways, roads in which comportments are inscribed. From my first meeting with most aspects of the world, I know how the human being is supposed to handle them; I am born into a world in which the roles I can play are written into institutions and held out to me in the very way people take care of me. "From the beginning of his life, the child proceeds by simply perceiving the kind of care that is given him and the utensils which surround him, to a deciphering of significations which inevitably generalize his personal drama into a drama of his culture" (*S*, p. 140).

In such a familiar world, each familiar role is known almost from the inside even before it is played; as in Commedia dell'arte each actor must express his personal genius within a traditionally structured framework, which his best inventions will in turn extend and transform for the generations to come. That man can and does succeed in expressing the individual, the strictly personal, aspects of his self is made possible precisely by the primordial humanity of the world's generalized intentions, structured for and by anonymous individuals. "Having first of all thought and lived according to what he thought good to do, and having perceived according to *l'imaginaire de sa culture* [the whole fund of generalized imagining power his culture offers him], he succeeds finally in reversing the relationship so that he is able to slide into the significations of his conduct and his words—to convert into culture—even that which is most secret in his experience" (S, p. 141). This necessity first to espouse the significations offered in order to make them ours and then, through their reconstruction, to influence the culture from which they come—this Sinngebung that is simultaneously centripetal and centrifugal—must be understood in order to comprehend the full thrust of Merleau-Ponty's declaration that the interior of our existence which phenomenology illumines is not a private life but "an intersubjectivity which links us ever closer to the whole history" (S, p. 141).

It is thus clear that any search for the truth of our Self—any quest for a valid ethic—must inevitably struggle with sociology and the meaning of history: The study of our liberty must involve us essentially in a description of our ingestion in the social-historical co-existence which is the world because being-in-the-world—existence—is for Merleau-Ponty first and foremost simply what it states. "When I realize that the social is not only an object, but first of all my situation," he writes in the Signs article devoted to the relationship of philosophy and sociology from which we have just been quoting, "and when I arouse in myself the awareness of this social existence which is mine, it is my entire synchronie which becomes present; it is, through it, all the past which I become capable of thinking as the synchronie which it was in its time" (p. 141). Philosophy is of course an effort to grasp the inner sense of man's existence; but if "the interior to which it leads us is not a private life but intersubjectivity which more and more intimately links us to the whole of history," then "the proper dimension of philosophy is that of coexistence" (S, p. 141). The search in myself for the traces of history goes hand in hand with the search in history for the key to myself, who am but power to reprendre and give sense to all my sedimented givens. The particular and the general must be played off against each other dialectically in the philosophical search for Being. It can only be found through the illuminating awareness of the individual's link and rapport with the whole of Being, that generality opened up by my existence, the only ground of universality.

This awareness has an existential end in the spirit of the classical

declaration that the truth will make you free. Just as a theory of
perception was necessary to understand the essential distinction between hallucination and true perception and thus to found criteria
for truth, so a theory of our insertion in the world must illumine the
individual's rapports with the social, with history. Only on the basis
of such a theory can I distinguish an act enjoying a legitimate social-
historical sense from an act of folly—in short, found criteria for right
and wrong.

The ontological importance of *Humanism and Terror* and *The
Adventures of the Dialectic*—essays superficially mistakable for mere
political commentary—cannot, against the background of these remarks, possibly be overlooked. From the war years until the end of
his life, Merleau-Ponty struggled to interpret the central problem
posed by Communism[2]—the sense in which the history of our time
is incarnated in the dispossessed class—and to grasp the future-form-
ing implications of the world-historical situation. In his efforts to
define phenomenologically the concrete terms in which a contemporary practica must work itself out, Merleau-Ponty incarnates brilliantly
the liberal conscience of contemporary Europe. *"Homme de gauche,"*
armed with aesthetic humanism, he is steeped in a philosophical tradition which, in various forms from Proust and Valéry to Heidegger
and Thomas Mann, has guided many who seek to make sense out of
a world that seems at one moment utterly senseless and at another
fated to sink under the weight of mankind's collective insensitivity.
In this regard Merleau-Ponty knows no superior for subtlety, complexity, and for the sincerity of a striving that, while passionate, is
stabilized by a genuine philosophical calm.

But the real philosophical significance of this struggle might be
missed in an overly clinical exposition. It is essential here to grasp
the full measure of the pathos characterizing the struggle of Merleau-
Ponty's hero. All creation is a molding of resistances: the artist must
through his reprise decenter and recenter what is offered, and the
poet, in forging a truly new expression, must espouse the proffered

2. The most informative short summary of the evolution of that struggle
is to be found in the most fascinating article ever written on Merleau-Ponty:
Sartre's memorial piece, "Merleau-Ponty Vivant," in the special issue of *Les
Temps Modernes* (17 [1961], 304–76) devoted to our author.

sense sedimented in the language and struggle to turn its weight in the direction he wants it to move. What the painter is to perception and the poet to the verbal generality, the hero is to the social-political order: he risks the struggle against the more immediate, more apparent resistances because he sees farther, recognizing their dependence on something deeper.

Merleau-Ponty was finishing *The Phenomenology of Perception* at a time when the sound of S.S. firing squads had not died away, and the existence of the hero—the reality of individuals somehow justified in offering their lives for a society and a history that seemed senseless, opposing what appeared at the moment to be the trend of history in the light of values they considered more important than the facts— was itself a fact. Indeed, the *Phenomenology* ends by insisting that philosophy must leave the last word to the hero. The task of philosophy is to help us see things—and historic situations—better; it can lead us to them, but then it must fall silent. For what is true of the poet, of the hero, indeed of every perceiver, is true of the philosopher: he must "allow Being itself to speak through us" (*S*, p. 225).

Thus, "It is true to say that [philosophy] realizes itself by destroying itself as separate philosophy" (*PP*, p. 520). Philosophy can tell us only of the general conditions of our insertion in the world, even its illumination of our concrete historical situation is abstract and therefore partial, stuck in a point of view untrue to the universal, dead, superstitious, and mystifying—unless the individual himself lives it. Only then can his natural and cultural body be able to go about its task of structuring a genuine field of action which alone can actually reveal in time, make present—actually make be—what is. Such a life is perforce paradoxical, inaccessible to description in rational, general terms. Indeed, in a sense it is impossible, while at the same time it is the only truly human vocation. It demands heroism, but heroism is the call of man, *cariatide du vide:* on the one extreme, he is called to full engagement, synchrony, risking loss of self-sufficiency in total communion with the Other (*S*, p. 245) and sacrificing his freedom through involvement in the historical process of sedimentation; on the other, he must abandon all security as he assumes full control, projecting the yet unknown future and therefore disentangling himself from the Other that already is. No man can avoid drinking to the dregs the loneliness resulting from the inescapable audacity that is the lot of the person who is, by birth, original. Nothing else could be expected of a being whose job it is to make sense out of the contingent, to incarnate truth in the present, to testify, as an individual, to the All. "But it is here that we must fall silent, for only the hero lives to the bitter end [*jusqu'au bout*] his relation to men and to the world; it is not proper that another speak in his name" (*PP,* p. 520). The last word of the *Phenomenology* is left to an authentic hero, Antoine de Saint-Exupéry, who, having literary gifts, also helped to clarify the nature of heroism:

> Ton fils est pris dans l'incendie, tu le sauveras. . . . Tu vendrais, s'il est un obstacle, ton épaule contre un coup d'épaule. Tu loges dans ton acte même. Ton acte, c'est toi. . . . Tu t'échanges. . . . Ta signification se montre, éblouissante. C'est ton devoir, c'est ta haine, c'est ton amour, c'est ta fidélité, c'est ton invention. . . . L'homme n'est qu'un noeud de relations, les relations comptent seules pour l'homme.[3]

Merleau-Ponty's silence did not last long, however, for there was still much to be inquired into—in that general way in which philosophy inquires—concerning that *noeud de relations.* By what signs does one recognize the authentic hero? What distinguishes him from the merely foolhardy martyr or from the genuinely courageous and even circumspect man who has mistakenly opposed the right or the good? Indeed, more fundamentally, how can one distinguish a good from a bad politique, the statesman from the opportunist?

These questions, already anticipated in the last pages of the *Phenomenology,* burn passionately throughout the essays in political philosophy which absorbed much of the philosopher's attention after the war. Though the essays stretch in time of composition from 1947

---

3. "Your son is caught in a fire, you will save him . . . if there is an obstacle you would sell your own shoulder for help from another shoulder. You are absorbed absolutely in your act. You *are* your act . . . you trade yourself . . . your meaning reveals itself, overwhelming. It's your duty, it's your hate, it's your love, it's your faithfulness, it's your discovery . . . man is but a bundle of relations, only the relations count for man." A. de Saint-Exupéry, *Pilote de Guerre,* pp. 171, 174, cited *PP,* p. 520.

(*Humanism and Terror*) through 1955 (*The Adventures of the Dialectic*) to the most recent of the "Propos" published in *Signs,* they are bound together by an ever-deepening inquiry into the questions of how the truth is incarnated in the political society and how, consequently, the active individual—whether politician or intellectual critic—must relate himself to it, must act in order to realize the truth. They reflect the evolution of Merleau-Ponty's position as regards Communism. The Berlin blockade and especially the invasion of South Korea struck him as aggressive acts that could no longer be interpreted as movements intended to defend the socialist lands against imperialist aggression and, hence, as signs that the dictatorship of the proletariat had hardened into another régime with illegitimate expansionist tendencies of its own. A deepening awareness of the implications of his own fundamental ontological position had already been leading him toward increasing distrust of all established dogmas. For our purposes, it is best to proceed directly to a presentation of the mature position, viewed precisely in terms of the underlying first philosophy.

REALIZING HUMANITY

At first reading, Merleau-Ponty's political essays might seem to lean on highly debatable assumptions in their struggle with what superficially appear to be problems posed by current events. Certain foundation stones of Marxist philosophy, for example, seem uncritically accepted as the horizons in which the discussion must unfold. In truth, however, the only assumptions are the positions of Merleau-Ponty's own philosophy that have been laboriously developed in *The Structure of Behavior* and *The Phenomenology of Perception*. In Marx, as in Freud and Saussure, Merleau-Ponty found vital discoveries, shrunk by too narrow a focus of interest, that almost cried out for the deeper ontological justifications a fundamental phenomenological philosophy could supply. Just as Freud's discovery in psychology of the concrete reality of incarnation and Saussure's discovery of the existential sense of language, so Marx's comprehension of man's essential symbiosis with his society, his discovery of the sense of history as the realization of humanity—"the recognition of man by man"—and his assertion that in our time sense is particularly incarnated in the unfulfilled aspirations of the dispossessed class are all truths that, to become really fruitful, require for their ultimate grounding the very principles of the *Phenomenology* and, reciprocally, give it body. It would be far better to realize that Merleau-Ponty attempted the fullest existentialization of Marx's early philosophy than to talk of his Marxism.

In order to understand the sense Merleau-Ponty gives to the Marxist formulation of the alternatives confronting mankind—social revolution or chaos—we must understand his ontological analysis of the grounding of truth in social situations and, hence, must turn again to *The Phenomenology of Perception*.

Beginning at the beginning, let us recall what distinguishes a "good"—a valid—perception from a "bad" one. A good perception is grounded in the opening of the space demanded correlatively by the thing and by the nature of the corps propre in order for the corps propre to obtain the grasp of the thing that permits the fullest and surest cooperation of Ego-thing. The role of the perceiver is essentially active: he moves out to the encounter with the thing, and the nature of his project influences the way the object is going to be made to stand there for him. The intentions offered by the world are revealed as they whirl into the dance of the body; they are structured as emotions and are given different senses in different contexts (the mountain, to use Sartre's example, is a thing of beauty to the tourist looking out from his well-heated chalet but a menacing obstacle to the men preparing to scale it to save a stranded climber). The inadequate perception brings the individual too close or too far or functions at too inhabitual an angle to permit as clear a grasp of the thing as can be achieved in circumstances that make the cooperation, the emotion, the "dance" possible.

Hallucinations and illusions, of course, are not inadequate perceptions because of their aggressiveness, their "activism"; they are errors, not imperfect truths. In every perception, it is true, there is an element of anticipation. The thing is fixed in the light of the new expression, the new cooperation that is to come, and anticipated data are presumed to fulfill the protensive intention. But illusions and hallucinations arise only when the anticipatory project is not sufficiently motivated by the intentions proffered in the field, not anchored. Especially in the hallucination, there is refusal of cooperation, rejection of the being calling for coexpression, as a sense that can lead to unactualized expression is imposed on a data that cannot flesh it out. The main source of hallucinations is the complex: instead of being truly opened to the actual solicitations of present givens, the subject remains obsessed by a part of the past that has failed to sediment properly—in other words, that has not allowed itself to be destructured and restructured in the natural movement of the subject's historical time. The complex must perforce clash with the enduring background solicitations that were given to the subject primordially with his corps propre: by illuminating only a part of his general humanity, it repels to the horizons much that normally would be coming to the fore in the course of time—hence, the strain.

The same pattern can be observed in political life. When social structures get frozen in reactionary decisions that run counter to the primordial and, as it were, eternal solicitations of Being; in other words, when they fail to call up the main conquests of man throughout history, from the basic most natural ones to their latest cultural extensions, and to expand them into new potentially fruitful institutions, then they begin functioning as complexes in the intersubjective world, rendering individuals and groups far less capable of responding to the demands of the present situation and of structuring it further. The man who here and now finds himself caught up in a whole intersubjective generalized system of such idolatrous counterhuman commitments (such as the whole capitalist property system) is often practically incapable of allowing the older more fundamental intentions, sedimentations of the most universal experience of mankind, to stand out through the tightly woven system of cultural ones. The most narrowly arbitrary considerations of individual or of class will motivate him to violent efforts to annihilate whatever traces of the fundamental givens he refuses to recognize—hence, for example, the kind of antisocial hysteria which reached enormous political dimensions at the end of the Third Reich. Ultimately, the most intellectual, most ideational, most reactionary or utopian projects are, by their very nature, the most violent. They tend to deafen the individual to the silent solicitations in the depths of the situation—those givens that come from birth and will survive even personal death because they are the ground limits and englobing atmosphere of humanity itself.

On the social level, then, as in personal existence opening to the given Other, *prise de conscience* and rejection of idols are the keys to valid action and the exercise of true freedom. Merleau-Ponty illustrates these considerations with the example of the revolutionary proletarian's prise de conscience in the historical moment of the revolution. The very possibility of the revolution was obviously incarnated in some sense in the situation and in the class that revolted; indeed, some common material condition must have motivated the workers and the tenant farmers to act as a class. But understanding the mode of that incarnation as an objective, material reality, as the Communists do, leads to acceptance of their conception of the Party, which, as spokesman for what is, can obviously do no wrong—a position that became increasingly difficult for a critical person to maintain the longer the Stalin régime endured.[4] A profusion of significations ("infrastructures" [*AD*, p. 265]) does in fact install each proletarian in an intersubjective situation prior to any prise de conscience, but they become objective factors he can handle—even if only by revolt and destruction—only when an external factor motivates the structuring of the space necessary to perceive them as the reality latent in the situation. If, as has been often remarked, revolutions usually occur after some rather substantial social progress has been offered to a group of people, it is because, like the animal who is entangled in the world of instincts and needs and who therefore lacks the mental space necessary for humanized perception, the proletarian is so totally absorbed in the moment-to-moment struggle to keep alive that he lacks the social space (*PP*, p. 507) in which to form the project necessary to perceive his situation. He is so caught in the present that he cannot *reculer dans l'avenir,* hope enough to form a project, or obtain sufficient grasp of his own integrity to recognize that of others and hence their capacity to be handled and

4. "If one concentrates all the negativity and all the sense of history in an existing historic formation, the proletarian class, then one must give *carte blanche* to those who represent it in power, for *every thing else is enemy.*" *AD,* p. 278.

cooperated with. Only when his social space becomes sufficiently structured to give him *du champ* can he ever be brought out of the direct condition of simply bearing his situation, "the thrust of a liberty without projects against unknown obstacles" (*PP*, p. 507). Not until projects are formed can obstacles be recognized as such.

It is interesting to witness the processes by which a man passes from simply living as an inevitability the conditions of the labor market which victimize him—including joblessness, weekly pay, lack of effective citizenship, and absence from his family—to conceiving of this inevitability as a revealing obstacle, an *Anstoss*. The worker discovers his rights by witnessing in action the affirmation of the rights of others, as a child discovers language by hearing others speak. He notes that the employees of another factory who used to live the same situation as his own now have won a difficult strike and that as their wages went up, his tended to follow. His situation suddenly seems less fatal and isolated. His class begins to recognize itself as intersubjective reality—as different yet coexistent with other classes —and the situation becomes revolutionary when the connections that do in fact exist among the members of the proletariat and between them and the rest of society are finally "lived in the perception of an obstacle common to the existence of each" (*PP*, p. 508).

The proletariat's first awakening to his situation is as "dumb" as the corps propre's first perception of its world. No express representation—no idea—is necessary to call up this feeling of solidarity in the common conviction, *ça doit changer!* The extraordinary effect of the *mots d'ordre* (watchwords) coming from those who spontaneously present themselves as leaders of the movement can be explained only by the fact of their truth to the intersubjective world which is waiting to be structured, to be expressed. Because they "crystallize what is latent in the life of all the producers," they are instantly obeyed, as if "by preestablished harmony" (*PP*, p. 508). They simply make explicit the solicitations of the sedimented *petites perceptions* which lie in all of Merleau-Ponty's "monads," tying them through their anonymous generality into the same world, as absorbing and total as the Leibnizian universe.

The parallels between this connection of the nature and importance of preconscious public opinion and Merleau-Ponty's continuous re-

assertion on all levels of the necessity to return to the original pre-
intellectual experience to found any truth, from the perceptual to
the artistic, are obvious. Here again, in Merleau-Ponty's terms, sense
can be tapped only if the primeval deposit of brute meaning is being
struck. Like the true idea, like the worthy hypothesis, the proper
decision which anticipatorily directs my action by crystallizing my
field of attention should be modeled on the lesson of the revolutionary
mot d'ordre's success. Both the true idea and the adequately deliberated
decision espouse as fully as possible the sense immediately proffered
by the world and give it focus in an expression that is adequate to
handle one's present situation as it is synchronically lived by other
subjects. I must "try to live naïvely what is offered me, without
trying to trick the logic of the enterprise, without locking it up from
the outset in the limits of a premeditated signification" (*AD*, p. 265).
The key to the true and the good is that *Hören auf dem Sein*—
Heidegger's virtue: listening to Being—in which Heidegger sees the
very essence of authenticity. Building my Self through the expressive
extension of the sense of my life is basically an act of *déchiffrement*—
my expression must decipher the sense of the situation latent in the
symbols through which it is represented to me and then must set
about realizing that sense through further development of the symbols. The genuine poet neither creates language out of nothing nor
repeats banally what has been always said. Similarly, the good
politique, like the good decision, is the one which will structure the
social field in a way that allows maximum play of all the soliciting
intentions without allowing any of these intentions to impede actualization and sedimentation of all others. Such indeed, as the *Signs*
essay on Machiavelli explains, is true humanist *vertu:* the Stoic expression must be understood in its deepest sense as advocating not
passive acceptance of what must be borne but actualization of what
must be, recognition of the latency of being, that which already really
is potentially presented in experience. In the political realm, vertu
is leading society to a realization of its potential self. It is opposed to
a sterile moralism whose fixed and abstract formulas represent the
horizons of an already crystallized past that has been lived by a highly
determined class. Such morality, like psychological sickness, falsifies
the effort to create a space for all the present pressures. The political

enterprise is one of risk and anticipation to be sure, "for the real is found only by going out ahead of it into the *imaginaire*" (S, p. 154). True vertu does not fear "dirty hands"; it is not above using trickery and honest hypocrisy in the interest of actualizing new structures, new institutions—figures whose capacity to crystallize the fond of the situation is still hypothetical and can be proven true and valid only if forced to come to be by a creative initiative. As all configurations, political institutions and political acts are of their essence ambiguous. Truths made of audacious guesses are destined to age soon into outworn clichés. And as is the case with all other expressive acts, the intersubjective political act—the establishment of new institutions—is a fumbling, awkward process: as the body's organs must learn gropingly to handle their objects, play their role, express themselves, under the Ego's leadership, so must the masses be brought to self-awareness—to world-awareness—by a process far from being angelic illumination. A certain amount of coaxing or forcing is inevitable; how much can be applied before the organ is destroyed is, of course, always the problem.

Political action is thus exceedingly dangerous, as is all decision, anticipation, stabilization, institutionalization, all cultivation of the individual, indeed all possession of whatever sort. "Whatever his good will may be, when man begins to act, he can never appreciate exactly the objective sense of his action; he constructs for himself an image of the future, justified only by probabilities; this image, guiding his actions, solicits the future on which very grounds it can be condemned, for the event itself once accomplished is not equivocal" (HT, p. 69). When I act, the field is structured, and the event as it occurs sediments immediately into a (partially) determining past. For that reason, it is easier to recognize an error retrospectively, in the light of the historically more structured situation, than it is to be certain prospectively that one is on the right course. I can never know my intention in acting until some time after the act, and sometimes I will never know. Merleau-Ponty has insisted on the inevitability of this "metaphysical hypocrisy": just as the presumption in perception renders the thing somewhat hallucinatory—its reality being tested only by its ability to withstand the pressure of the intersubjective world of action—so in moral life any assertion of intentions, any decision, will be recognizable as valid only by its capacity to be repeated and assimilated as history ebbs and flows about it. If I declare and believe that I am unconditionally *quoi que ce soit,* I am ignoring the principle of metaphysical hypocrisy, expressive of the finitude of my insertion in the world. But since every action on my part inevitably forces me to take a stand, to behave, in order to confront the unequivocal event as though I also really were unequivocally this or that, metaphysical hypocrisy is indeed inevitable.

We cannot avoid dangerous choices by declaring, like the Parisian concierge *"Je ne fais pas de politique."* No man can be apolitical. "Whatever the surprises of the event, we can no more do without prediction and consciousness than without our body" (*S,* p. 276). The ontological sense of Pascal's *"Nous sommes embarqués"* is the same as that of Merleau-Ponty's discovery that the only way of resolving the paradox of existence is simply to exist—Achilles needs only to run in order to catch up with the tortoise. Only by ever-renewed essays at social restructuring, by risking the projection of new social forms, can the politician make possible a valid politics, for it is only when a stand is taken, and thus a field is structured, that the dumb, latent forces can stand out, articulate themselves one upon another, and explicitly take up a sense.

It is all very well to declare the need for risk, of course, but one must be able somehow to distinguish the necessary, justifiable risk from imprudent foolhardiness. It is not enough to reply that the leader, in taking the risk of action, must be guided by the givens of the situation, for, considering the inevitable ambiguity of the givens, he must still be able to distinguish a policy of superficial opportunism from action that really moves in function of the most inclusive and profound (i.e. respectful of the most primordial, most general sedimentations of our humanity) reading of the tension, resistances, solicitations, and possibilities that can be obtained. Merleau-Ponty, contemplating the life of Machiavelli, delivers a judgment that suggests what is needed to direct a fruitful politique: Despite his remarkable anticipation of humanism's true needs, Machiavelli lacked a *fil conducteur*—an Ariadne's thread—"which would have permitted him to recognize, between various powers, the one of whom there was something to be hoped, and to elevate without question vertu above opportunism" (S, pp. 280–81). This notion of fil conducteur—the demand of humanity to realize itself, to structure its world, which is held out to us as the guide, the only authentic alternative to chaos— is thus evidently an important one in Merleau-Ponty's Practica. He offers, in Signs, two illustrations of it. Machiavelli at times seemed to sense what could have been his Ariadne's clew—the need for over- coming the fragmentation of Italy and for expelling the foreigner so that some sort of stable human communication interior to the penin- sula could ultimately become possible. Another illustration, central to the case with which the whole Practica is concerned, is the Marx- ist notion of the rule of the proletariat. The tightly knit web of com- munications that now unite the world suggested to Marx this fil conducteur which continues to animate Communist political thought and is central to Merleau-Ponty's political philosophy. The notion of the proletariat provided Marx with "the algebraic formula of revolu- tion" (S, p. 350) and thus of history itself.

A social-economic class can offer the political leader ontological grounds to lift policy above opportunism because, being totally dis- possessed, the proletariat is not hardened by arbitrary projects born of the desire to retain possessions. It thus remains in direct contact, however dumb and formless the contact may be, with the fullness of primordial reality. In such a class, nothing obstructs symbiosis with the generality of the anonymous "ON," which, in the form of hu- manity's most general sedimentations, provides, in social relations as in perception, the horizons of truth, the standard for action. Pre- cisely because of its generality, such a standard contrasts with the superficial and narrowly personal bonté of the morality mouthed by those with limited vested interest.

> The proletariat, which has no earthly goods, no interests, almost
> no positive traits, is ready for this very reason to play a universal
> role. It is by essence revolutionary . . . but it does not know
> itself; it has no idea of the means, of the episodes, or of the
> institutions through which it will express what Marx calls "the
> secret of its silence." The Party's role will be to transform its
> revolt into long-lasting positive action. The party incarnates the
> revolt, destroys it in its immediacy, thus becoming negation of

the negation; in this fashion, the class that negates becomes the class that founds. (S, p. 350)

The key to history, imperfectly grasped by Machiavelli, here finds its fullest expression. The most general human experience must be allowed to assume fully its place as ground of authentic intersubjectivity. The Party's program appeals to all men when it expresses in proper structures the common fond of humanity sedimented in us by a long historical tradition. The proletariat's generality provides the Party with its matter just as the corps propre's generality provides the matter of perception. The proletariat's need, its *néant*, is the source of its creative richness, for it lives the world with some degree of that immediacy and primordial anonymity that permits the corps propre to found the real. Its dumb cry to be torn from this unbearable immediacy is its call for temporally unfolding expression and crystallization in the cultural body; this ever-evolving self-expression is actualized through the cultural organ of the Party, which, in a sense, serves as its Cogito. The Party, however, can continue to structure valid social forms only so long as it remains in intimate contact with the mute reality lived in the primordial given, the proletariat's existential experience of the world.

The ontological reasons why it is difficult, indeed almost impossible, for the Party to establish such contact are clear. Any and every anticipatory risk that fails to englobe in the field it structures all the real intentions the world is holding up to it becomes, like the complex, idolatrous and enslaving, a *non-sense* tending toward the violence of terror (S, p. 281).

Against the background of this terrifying perspective, the necessity for the régime constantly to renew its effort to keep communication open (S, p. 281) is obvious. True communion between Party and masses is indispensable to its unceasing effort to structure social forms that bring all the intentions in the social world to expression. Merleau-Ponty does not condemn the leaders of the Russian Revolution as incompetents or power-hungry madmen for their failures at this. Rather, his analysis of this most significant example aims at showing the extreme difficulty of such a task. The very first lie told to the proletariat sediments a debilitating tradition that begins to lock the

Party up in itself. The result is *mépris*—the master's *méconnaissance* of the Other and hence of himself (*S*, pp. 275, 276). The road back to communication is from then on a very dangerous one. When de-Stalinization unleashes the powers of criticism against the stability of the régime, it leaves an open wound in the side of the body politic, but a wound that cannot, must not, be avoided. "The dictatorship is asked to call itself into question [*se contester*] and to let itself become eliminated; the proletariat is asked to liberate itself and to reject the control of the dictatorship. This is difficult, almost impossible. The world has only the choice between that way and chaos" (*S*, p. 378).

Thus, even though the generality of the mass is a source of political possibility, it introduces an element of danger into every actualization of that possibility on the part of the leadership. To command this mass, the leader has only a few gestures and words, which come as the pronunciamentos of an almost legendary figure to his "mute spectators caught up in the vertigo of a life *à plusieurs* (*S*, p. 275). The leader's geste is like a flame that is picked up by a million mirrors, each reflecting each other, until it becomes a brilliant aura scarcely resembling the initial point. Reflected and dispersed through many monads, it is stripped of all idealistic guarantee of exactness.

Given this reality, the leader's objectives must be as clear as the means for accomplishing them are obscure: "Through his domination of his relations with the Other, the man in power overcomes the obstacles between man and man and puts some transparence in our relations—it is as though men can be close only in a sort of distance" (*S*, p. 275). In short, he must carry out the disposition of social space (*l'aménagement de l'espace social*). The acts of the leader are like the expressive act's *recul dans le néant* in that they differentiate the great general mass by polarizing and structuring in order to create the distance, *le pli dans l'être,* the wave on the surface of the great ocean of Being, that permits Being to become aware of itself. If the leader allows his acts to become lost in the all-reflecting maze, as an aura that brings no glance of self-recognition to either the individuals who make up the field's points of resistance or the leader himself, if he fails to dramatize a project in which the vast majority can find definite roles while he retains his own freedom and lucidity in the process, then the great forces that are really but ambiguously present in the society will either go undirected or be falsely forced, will remain amorphous or be repressed. The *force de l'âme* of Machiavelli's Prince is the resoluteness, directed by a veritable *Hören auf dem Sein* necessary to bring such a field-structuring into being. "It is a question —between the will to please and défiance, between self-complacent goodness ('a soft way of ignoring the Other and therefore *de le mépriser*') and cruelty—of conceiving a historical enterprise in which all can join." Again, truth is expression, and expression cooperation —"the dance in common."

There is no eternal solution to the political problem of creating social forms that will keep communication open through self-expression (any more than there can be a book to end all books, a painting that says all that painting has to say, or a final science). The dialogue must go on forever as oppositions renew themselves and differentiations and syntheses continue to well up in the dynamic continuity of tradition; such is the law of expression, of all structuring of a field; such is the nature of sense, temporal direction. That continuity is made possible by both the given historical necessity of the human situation and the resoluteness of the virtuous hero who recognizes its demands and acts consistently in view of it.

Is Merleau-Ponty's description of the *fil conducteur* itself sufficiently strong to serve as "the word" which can structure our fields of action? Is it real enough to structure a resoluteness against false alternatives, steadfastly clear enough to hold fast the hero even unto death? When he rejects the notion of a human nature conceived as a fixed unequivocal idea in favor of a historical becoming without predetermined goal, the signs of which, at a given moment in history, are acts tending to improve and express communion between men, his philosophy certainly gains in flexibility (hence political realism) what it loses in rigor, which is extremely attractive. But the guideposts to authenticity may be so unstructured that they cannot contain or sufficiently restrain the calculated tricks, the necessary "hard" acts to which all leaders must apparently have recourse. Merleau-Ponty condemns torture (*S*, p. 408) and holds the lie to be the sign par excellence of the beginning of political failure (*PP*, p. 372); such acts certainly do manifest, on the part of those who commit them, a *mépris* which is nothing but a *méconnaissance* of what is human in themselves as well as in the Other. But, realistically and practically, some negation of the negation, some hard overcoming of hardened complexes, some dangerous planning must be admitted as inevitable. A philosophy which, in order to describe our finitude, has recourse to contradiction and installs violence at the very heart of even the perceptive and intellectual acts finds it difficult to determine the exact lines separating justifiable from unjustifiable violence.

Merleau-Ponty is therefore fascinated by the questions raised in cases like those of Bukharin (*HT*, passim) and Trotsky (*S*, pp. 309–28) or the war in Algeria, where individuals and groups are sacrificed in the name of the public good. If the obstructing opposition or the Party member who has failed to read the situation cannot be brought to authentic, spontaneous *autocritique,* to voluntary abnegation, to synthesis and communion, what should or can be done? When it becomes known that fourteen million Russians are confined in labor camps, the Stalin case is undoubtedly closed. But, although "every régime has its internees" (*S*, pp. 330–36; 339–43), at what point does it go beyond a mere overcoming of the points of hardened, false opposition to unqualified terror and a new form of idolatry? How can those who refuse communion, who will always pit naked will against the good of others in order to hang onto privileges, be brought into line? How can any line ever be proven to have been the right one?

Success of some kind is the basic standard here, though Merleau-Ponty repeatedly asserts that raw success is not the criterion for the truth of a politique (*HT*, pp. xxx–xxxi). A prince who is doing exactly what will favor the development of humanity in his principality can be destroyed—from the outside—by hostile, less authentic powers (*S*, p. 275), while a perfectly inhuman power may gain a temporary success through a combination of lying to the people, appealing to their complexes, and sheer terror. Nevertheless, had the Thousand-Year Reich succeeded in fulfilling its announcement, it would have had to change:

> In order to be a politique, Nazism would have had to give itself new watchwords, to find present justifications, to insinuate itself into existing forces; otherwise, after fifty years of Nazism, it would be nothing but a memory. A legitimacy that does not

find the means of proving its worth and getting accepted as valid
(*se faire valoir* [ambiguous here]) perishes in time, not that
the one which takes its place then becomes venerable and holy,
but that the new system constitutes from then on the fond of
beliefs incontested by the majority that only the hero dares
contest. (*HT*, p. xxxi)

The undesirable ambiguity of this declaration is painfully obvious.
Indeed, the whole of *The Adventures of the Dialectic* and the political
essays collected in the last section of *Signs* are devoted to developing
the sense of the fil conducteur—the realization of humanity—beyond
this confusion until it becomes capable of operating as a proper guide.
Has the effort been successful? The suggestion that we need to re-
examine, as expression of possible complexes, glib assertions of
"individualism," "personality," "race," "high society," is valid, like
the point that it is meaningless to assert that humanity can become
permanently inhuman (what, then, does "human" mean?); but it is
unfortunate that nothing in the notion of humanity that Merleau-
Ponty's historical existentialism describes can really handle the question of success which the preface to *Humanism and Terror* so per-
tinently raises (not to mention the greater problem of the individual's
practical and concrete relationship with the régime). The theoretical
demarcations are not unequivocal enough to forestall the possibility
of a wily, flexible, unscrupulous régime's compromising with the deeper exigencies of the corps propre by espousing them just enough to
stall off—perpetually—the need for open revolt, while it continually
sediments into the general soul a base culture deliberately designed
to deaden the urge to develop what is most personal and most human
in the individual.

Merleau-Ponty's last word on this question is that success is no
accident but an *avènement,* an accession; there is, for him, no fatum
—no necessary destiny—but neither does he see the contingency of
history as senseless. Rather, the spirit of history is Fortuna, and since
"Fortune is a woman," seduction is, with her, the only mode of true
coexistence; such coexistence, as conceived in terms of his rethought
Freudianism, is the standard of success. The man who has not grown
from the extreme master-slave relationship characteristic of child-

hood to the mature acceptances of the adult can hardly be said to be living. Mature sexuality, born of the respectful and creative cooperation of an authentic couple in constant evolution, alone allows each pole of the relationship to find full identity, full self-expression, in the common adventure. Such sexuality based on seduction is the age-old symbol of man's relation to the world and, singularly, of the hero's relation to his country, to the masses he must help inform in the creation of the new institutions that will bind them to himself in common self-expression. In the political world, as in the sexual world, terror is the failure of seduction; hence it is doomed. Only the politics that respect and bring out into expression what is deepest in the incarnated situation—that appeal to the social world sexually in this truly human sense—can succeed. Such politics alone allow both leader and masses really to come to be in harmonious consciousness, in moments of truth where each becomes and loses himself in true rapport.

The problem is, however, that, if the woman is riddled with complexes, the kind of seduction that appeals to her will often seem to be practically the most successful one; similarly, sedimentation of a bad history can prepare a country to respond to abominable solicitations on the part of the astute demagogue. When wooing either, how can one ever be sure of what one is appealing to and whether the response —or, worse, the lack of it—is due to the inauthenticity of the appeal or to that of the body that is answering?

In any case, Sartre, in *Situations, IV,* leaves little doubt that Merleau-Ponty personally became deeply disenchanted with his own capacity to seduce the history of France in the postwar years. This portrait (*TM,* pp. 332ff.) helps us realize the full significance of Merleau-Ponty's silence on political matters and his return to inquiry into the mute forms of expression.

One of his last descriptions of the evolution of human structures, in an article commenting on the new social anthropology of Claude Lévi-Strauss (*S,* pp. 143–57), suggests a certain dissatisfaction with the enduring forms the humanization of man has taken. The remarks center about that most fundamental coexistential relation, marriage: where primitive man tended, through incest prohibitions, simply to go against nature in his effort to liberate himself from the immediacy of its demands, the societies that have achieved the enterprise of modern history have transformed it by guile, have composed with it, achieving, through their reprise of it, "a series of mediations in which the structure never emerges altogether as pure universal." The development of evermore flexible symbolic systems, inviting "each man to define his own system of exchange," may indeed offer much more efficacious possibilities, but such systems are less beautiful, less hieratic, than earlier forms of expression. Merleau-Ponty echoes Heidegger's regret at the "desacrilization" (one of his rare but important references to the *Heilige*), and his objections to "the altogether profane usage of life, accompanied indeed by little compensatory myths without depth" (*S*, pp. 154–57) recall Heidegger's attack on *Kultur*.[5]

Much more unmistakable is the condemnation in "L'Œil et l'esprit" —Merleau-Ponty's last published article—of activism, which is presented as virtually the central form of modern life. It certainly seems to have succeeded very well—in the sense of having "become accepted, taken over, and lived": wherever we turn rises the specter of the United States, inhuman to be sure (as in all leftist French literature) and universally imitated, so that even Russia itself is beginning to resemble it like a brother. Everywhere, activism—the fascination with a strange kind of creativity, of practical violence, of senseless change, with such slogans and watchwords as "what will work," "how can it be made to work?" and "nothing succeeds like success"—challenges the philosopher to call man back to an awareness of "the true and the false," to the "primordial givens of his situation." He must point to the humanity which has made history possible, to the *historicité primordiale,* even to the prestructured, not yet artificial Being. This is a grave, difficult task, especially when the philosopher has previously denied the reality of a human nature and of the corresponding ethical necessities and has affirmed in their stead an inexpressible unconscious, betting on humanity's Fortuna as standard bearer. It is disturbing to find the philosopher of intersubjectivity and total engagement turning with nostalgia to the painter's silent, solitary experiments as closer to the real than anything he or anyone else can say.

5. Heidegger, *Holzwege* (Frankfurt/Main, Klostermann, 1950), pp. 93–94.

But the difficulties in Merleau-Ponty's Practica are clearly not mere self-generated problems arising from the neglect of some simple order of facts or from errors of logic. As genuine philosophy, it confronts us with the human problem as such, expressed according to the accents and rhythms proper to the particular space the philosopher's vision has been able to open for us. Its declarations that the primitive myth, the Oedipus complex, and the neurosis—"an individual myth"—(S, p. 152) are more than irrelevant curiosities are profoundly correct, but disagreement on the most fundamental ontological level must arise when it suggests that the very enterprise of truth, the very possibility of human experience, resides in a fundamental contradiction, a paradox which can be lived only by dialectically moving on.

Thus the Practica can do no more than indicate where we must finally search for the grounds of an existential ontology—namely, in the poetic conception of aestheticism, an epistemological-ontological approach resembling the Heideggerian conception of truth as *Aletheia,* a veiling-unveiling. On this most basic level, Merleau-Ponty's descriptions have a high degree of phenomenological sophistication and a far-ranging sweep of application. Our critical reconsideration will have to begin by looking to them for the perceptive grounds on which clearer demarcations can be drawn than the Practica seems able to justify.

CHAPTER 5

Poetica: A New Montaigne

BEING AND EXPRESSION

As IN THE PRECEDING CHAPTERS, the central problem proposed by Merleau-Ponty's philosophy—or, more exactly, the peculiar formulation his vision gives to the eternal philosophical problem—outlines itself fairly clearly. The questions of truth and liberty—the inquiry into the possibilities for the right and proper direction of my existence —depend ultimately on the ontological problems of the exact sense of my being-in-the-world. Let us briefly summarize the implications of the previous discussion, first from the standpoint of the individual (What is my relationship to the world in which I have to make my way?), then from the standpoint of the world (What does the All achieve through individualization?).

Let us turn first to a vital instance of our role as founders of truth, the practical problem of the position of the individual in relation to the massive political situation in which he is caught up. Here, the danger of loss of self is evidently present at opposite extremes, which we may term, curtly, fascination (or opportunism), and activism (or terrorism). Failure to structure or control a situation, fanatic adherence to a movement, all exploitations of it, including drifting along with it, are forms of fascination: such passive absorption in one's world, far from reflecting full creative communion with it, presupposes a refusal to relate oneself fully to the situation, to appreciate it for itself, to respect it. Ironically, the individual who thus makes no effort to understand the deeper demands of his present world neglects himself as well; he misses the opportunity to respect himself in turn, for the deeper truth of the situation is in him, as corps propre, and the fullest realization of its possibilities—of his own potentialities—is dependent upon his being able to structure properly what otherwise would remain an amorphous mass of general possibilities sedimented as a potential fond for an unrealized series of fruitful figures. At the opposite extreme stands the overactive individual who feverishly crystallizes ever-new figures on the surface of the same general ground, by which in truth he is just as blindly motivated, on which in fact he depends as totally as his more passive counterpart, the essential difference being that he constantly dissimulates the fact even to himself. In trying to dominate the situation absolutely, the activist commits the same sin of disrespect as the fascinated. Both fail to root their Selves and their world in the given situation opened by their "being there." Both fail to recognize the bipolar nature of all reality. Ignoring the ground and the limits of his point of view and the ambivalent sense of the structures he would mold the situation to, the activist, like the fascinated, is lost to himself as he plunges ahead to realize his ideal. Indeed, no one is so lost to himself as the dictator blinded by the ideational transparency—by the halo—of his own cult of personality.

Fascination-activistic formalism: these are the *Grenze* (the limits in the Heideggerian sense) and, in their extremes, the temptations of human existence. Caught between opportunism and terrorism, between consuming passion and cold eroticism, between Dadaist spontaneity and dry stylism, between the child's enchanted garden and the man's manipulation of others, between oriental *rêverie* and occidental analytic thought, between myth and scientism; in one illness unable to keep things "out there" in space, so that buildings fall over him, in another, hallucinatorily projecting snakes that do not exist, man is trapped finally between the Spinozistic dream (*S,* p. 187) to become one with the All and find a truth stripped of all limits and the technician's desire to be in full possession of his limited kingdom. Human expression runs the full gamut of these extremes, from the vague immersion of music (*TM,* p. 195) to the dominating *survol* of mathematics.

After the rather overwhelming vision of these extremes, where can salvation he found? This is the purport of Merleau-Ponty's last published work, *Signs*. As the Preface tells us, *Signs* is devoted to the search for flashes of signification, for those privileged moments when human expression in any field of action makes existence possible through the institution and sedimentation of meaning and thus (as seen from the transcendental viewpoint) makes Being be. *Signs* is a search for every kind of *reprise d'un acquis* in the acts of seeing, speaking, and understanding through which we build ourselves, the world, and each other. For such signals alone offer clues to the answer why "there is something rather than nothing at all." The political studies previously mentioned—indeed all the instances presented in *Signs,* whether drawn from sociology, philosophy, political commentary, or criticism of the arts—are thus to be taken as "philosophical exercises," in the sense of "spiritual exercises." They are mere *ébauches* to be filled in by the reader, whose cooperation with their solicitation is essential; essays in Montaigne's sense, outlines in the ontology of proper distance which invite us to essay ourselves the exercise of a living thought which is neither *survol* nor mere unfigured *rêverie.*

The theme of *Signs* is symbolism viewed as "the ruse with Being," the poetic art of placing institutions between us and the All, which protective shield alone makes possible our authentic individuality. That individuality can survive only by recognizing, in the heart of its uniqueness, its ground in the All and hence its dependence on the Other; in turn it is what makes possible the manifold dialogue in which Truth and Being come to be. Merleau-Ponty's philosophical quest culminates in this effort to pursue Being in its own domain, to look for its secret "in the symbolic function, source of all reason and all unreason," to make a step in the founding of that "rigorous theory of symbolism" the absence of which he deplores (*S,* pp. 153, 244). It is always as *lieu de la fission de l'Etre,* as result, deposit, and trace of a *déhiscence de l'Etre* that Merleau-Ponty studies the symbol, the institution, the classic, for they are the very body of "that unique activity of rendering explicit and signifying which we ourselves are." All the images that the poet-philosopher weaves around the symbolic activity to give it outline converge toward this notion: "transparent wall," "edge in Being," "zone-marker," "proliferation woven between men in which things can stick," *"fulguration figée,"* "pyramid" (whose base is the corps propre's generality and whose summit is the point of expression), "instrument"—the symbol, the successful figure, is always that which can separate while uniting, render invisible Being present as a certain absence, liberate by rooting, sustain an other while effacing itself, and permit an opening in order that it can then demand to be filled. Accumulation of all our sedimented symbols, *la culture bienveillante et traîtresse,* mother and daughter of brute Being and *la pensée sauvage,* is the locus of all mediation, transcendence, and coexistence. Authentic culture is that "receptacle of tolerant givens" which permits us to engage ourselves without fascination, to choose and accept forms of Being as qualified, to recognize that all sets of values, perfectly valid though they may be, eventually can, and should, be replaced by others (*PP,* p. 516). Rather than figures forever closed in upon themselves, true culture proposes "modes of universal engagement," variations on the theme of existence which at once indicate that other variations are possible and thus sustain the individual's power to pull free of any given moment, of any particular structure, by the assertion of ever-new figures. It is in this sense that we must understand that "my liberty is in things" (*PP,* p. 516), and that the things are "caught up in the web of culture."

It is not surprising that these exercises in the ontology of proper distance concentrate on the active "ruse with Being" itself rather than on the fascination which occurs when it fails. But the threat is always present, as a reminder not only of what can happen when culture fails but, more tragically, that there is never any guarantee that it will not. "The possibility always remains of an immense compromise, of a *pourrissement de l'histoire,* of history becoming rotten." Similarly, the ruse of language can push back only for a moment the *maléfice du social,* that play of mirrors which is the intersection of our looks (*S,* pp. 258, 385); thus, the very idea of an expression which succeeds is permanently called into question. But even if the successful ruse's conquest is merely temporary, the philosopher must seek to understand the rule of its success, why the endurance of the classic as opposed to the destruction and chaos wrought by that activism which endangers the very existence of Western culture.

If these remarks concerning the art of the individual's maintaining liberty for himself in his coexistence with the All do not make clear enough the importance of mastering that art and its rules, consideration of the problem from the other angle, poetically, will perhaps drive home the sense of the difficult synthesis Merleau-Ponty proposes, a dialectic which respects both the One and the Many, universal truth and individual points of view. As Sartre remarks in his memorial article, one gets the feeling in reading Merleau-Ponty not that there is no God, but that God needs men. Although this way of putting it is obviously foreign to the transcendental point of view which remained Merleau-Ponty's, the human tone with which it speaks of the terror of this philosophy is nevertheless justified. Merleau-Ponty's conviction that Being has torn itself apart to produce consciousness, through which it would possess itself reflectively, stems from the principal stalk of occidental philosophy; but, from the viewpoint of the idealism in classical positions, his denial that this self-possession is achieved first, foremost, or ever in a pure total reflection is uniquely skeptical. The impossibility of a transparent exhaustive grasp of anything is to Merleau-Ponty the indication par excellence that it is Being itself which is revealed in human perception. Truth comes to self-possession only through the reflection of many individual moments in time; existence opens man onto the totality of Being, but only from a point of view, and Being must therefore present itself to us as hidden in the most part, although in itself essentially discoverable. The paradoxical belief that each of our worlds is a *partie totale de l'Etre* explains Merleau-Ponty's preference for the antinomies of visible and invisible, illumined and opaque, rather than real and unreal, true and false, or être and néant. If any Cogito's apparent self-grasp is necessarily dependent on its contingent ground in the essentially opaque whole, then any assertion of full, enduring transparency and autonomy must be an illusion, a misuse of the finite transcendental anticipatory power that Being has achieved for itself. Such a surge forward loses its grip on both its essential nature and its purpose.

Sartre points to moments of "teleological excess" here, but it must be understood that Merleau-Ponty has explicitly recognized a Bergsonian teleology in the Husserlian conception of *Fundierung*.[1] Teleology, when thus understood, is then not anathema to him. The relation between Being and a particular moment of consciousness is inevitably bipolar; its sense is founded by the very relation itself. The active pole can be considered to be working for the lower, but it could not function without this lower, the fundamental, which calls for it as its development, its expression. This is teleology only in this exact sense: though the higher is for the sake of the lower, it obviously can be neither reduced to nor deduced from the lower, for it is really something other. To the question of why Being has instituted for itself the possibility of a finite, human reflection on itself, there is, of course, no answer, but in a clear understanding of the implications of the simple fact that it has done so can be found the key not only to the fullness of life but to bare human survival.

That the surge forward, the "crest of the wave," the *pli dans l'Etre*, the *recul dans l'avenir*, which makes possible the privileged moment's turning back on the whole in order to take it in hand and guide it to fuller realization of itself, can, unfortunately, separate itself and thus begin to destroy itself through its uprootedness and false self-direction is, of course, a danger inherent in its being higher. Not only is the threat of activism ever-present, but, as we have already hinted and shall demonstrate more adequately later, a certain "as if," an inevitable "metaphysical" hypocrisy, is an important element in the very nature of the enterprise, part of the paradox of self-extending finitude. Because the highest moment is grounded, however, the opposite danger, fascination, remains to threaten it at the other extreme.

The attempt to grasp the art of the proper and fruitful "ruse with Being," to the extent it lies in any way under our control (which attempt, because it holds the key to fullest existence, is the very task of phenomenological philosophy) must consider in this ontological light the various forms of ruse, of "opening a space," that permit founded-reflective guidance of the intersubjective destiny of man. We

1. "There is finality only in the sense in which Heidegger has defined it, when he said, approximately, that it is the trembling of a unity exposed to contingency and which untiringly creates itself. It is to the same spontaneity, undeliberated, inexhaustible, to which Sartre alluded when he said that we are 'condemned to liberty.'" *S*, p. 122.

shall seek to gain a precise understanding of what is authentic about their proper use and unartful in their abuse.

First arises, naturally, the question, Is there a central form that is basically characteristic of the human comportment; is there hence a kind of ruse par excellence in terms of whose highest achievement all the others should be understood? We need not hesitate to declare that expression is the mode in which the human world institutes itself and that culture is simply the accumulation of expressive power, but whether we can go a step further and signal language as the highest form of expression is more problematic. Merleau-Ponty's vocabulary and imagery seem to point in this direction: Gestures "speak"; thought is an "interior dialogue"; perception is sometimes characterized as a dialogue in which things finally find a voice, and we are told history might lose its sense like a "sentence that one drops without concluding it." Brute Being is dumb as it waits to be disenchanted, and truths, when finally expressed, seem to say what "Being wished to say forever, *depuis toujours*."

There is, in fact, something privileged about language. The word accumulates expressive power with unusual plasticity and possibility of cross-reference, making it possible to transcend the sign toward the sense (*dépasser le signe vers le sens*). Language has thus an extraordinarily transparent referential and reflective power. This transparency gives rise to the very venture of Truth and to the illusion of the pure Idea, which suggests of course that language may not be as privileged a form of expression as first appeared. The very superiority of language is also what makes it dangerous; language makes activism possible. The more silent (*muettes*) forms of expression are necessary to recall us to order, for in them, above all in painting, the ground of our sense-giving in Being is more manifest.

To clarify these relationships, we must return to the primitive reality of expression as such and recognize in it the kind of stance which permits the center of initiative—ultimately the conscious man—to structure a figure in Being. Only then can we elaborate the special expressive powers of language and properly contrast its potentially activistic qualities with the potentially fascinating characteristics of painting, so that the ultimate existential sense and the validity of both can be appreciated.

THE MOST BASIC EXPRESSION: THE GESTURE

The primordial medium of all expression is the body. With every movement the body not only can but *must* express; as it is the seat of an existence, each of its poses, even the abandon of sleep, is always significant. Now a gesture can be more or less voluntary, more or less spontaneous—on the one hand, a grimace of horror, or, on the other, the reaching for an apple—but the most spontaneous is not the least expressive. On the contrary, the reverberations of such an action are perhaps less precise but also less limited. From the shaking of a fist to the focusing of the eyes in vision, the gesture is always an effort to adapt oneself to the situation and the situation to oneself or, better, to bring both together in a meaningful, manageable configuration.

Previously successful *mises en forme* of this type remain generally inscribed in the body as habits, memories, abilities, always ready to be recombined in new ways according to the individual's style of dialogue with the world. They serve as his shield against the world and his instrument for handling it. In fact, they provide the very stage on which his battle is to be fought. Whenever the body moves to take an attitude, a meaning is incarnated in matter, a sense inscribed in things, so that anyone who witnesses a particular gesture will immediately recognize its meaning and the sense it casts on the surrounding world. Within the totality of the material world, the gesture brings about a certain polarization as it sketches out in space a comportment which radiates a signification that modifies the sense of the whole world for those present.

That expression is the ground of all transcendence and intentionality has already been indicated by the descriptions in the *Phenomenology* of how I am in space, in what sense I inhabit a world "with" other things. When I reach out for a desired object, it is not "over there" (and I "over here") in a point of an objective space without reference; rather, it presents itself within a system. It is desirable and reachable, as it were, by an internal connection to the body as reacher. Hence in order to bring thing-there and body-here together, I do not have to compose concepts or miraculously command all the complicated physical mechanisms of body, thing, motion, or spatiality.

The thing is no foreign body; it is already acting as a pole in a dynamic system of prise, structured in my field as thing-graspable-to-be-grasped. In view of the fact that it is by virtue of my intention of reaching out for it that it is made to stand there as reachable, the wonder is that I can explicitly distinguish reached-for object and reaching subject at all. Such a distinction is not necessary to the success of this reaching operation, and indeed there is no reason to suppose that any such reflexive opposition occurs in animals.

Now precisely because it expresses a relationship to the world that implies some distinction between the one gesturing and the situation gestured about, the primordial human gesture contains in seed all the characteristics of more sophisticated acts of expression. It inscribes itself through the body immediately into the "stuff" of the world, where it becomes a kind of line of force or of polarization that is significant. Moreover, it can be *repris,* imitated; its sense can then be further reflected on, both by its author and its witnesses.

Its special significance—the transcendental unity of two moments achieved in the opposition of subject and situation—radiates beyond itself and suggests innumerable possible variations of gestures or reaches and of objects desirable or undesirable, obtainable or presently unobtainable. It incarnates the individual's attitude of the moment without freezing him or exhausting his personality and possibilities in the process; it summarizes his situation without pretending finally to explain the world on which it is meant to be only a momentary hold and into which it opens many possible new perspectives. True to the end of expression, as such, it liberates the individual from the power of the particular instant by "instituting it" (as Hegel says of *Gewöhnheit* in the *Encyklopedia*), by solidifying it into a jumping-off point from which and with the help of which he will be able to move further in one of the directions sketched out by its success or failure. As we shall see, the word results from the maximum exploitation of these possibilities.

Something more than the minimal animal behavior is necessary to explain the special significance that the world acquires through human expression. For example, although animal comportment transforms the physical world, making "food" appear here, "a hiding place" there, and thus "giving to the stimuli a sense they did not have" (*PP,*

p. 221), this *Umwelt* nevertheless seems narrow and relatively stable; as Koffka puts it, it lacks plasticity, for the animal seems fascinated by the objects which are meaningful for him and is therefore unable to interest himself in those aspects of things which are not typical in terms of the characteristic forms he gives his environment. Indeed, the forced introduction of unassimilable stimuli, as in laboratory experiments, can readily lead to the production of neuroses like those Pavlov observed in his dogs (*SC*, pp. 56f.). The animal is apparently so unable to recognize further potential meaning in typical objects of his interest, to see them as rich opaque selves packed with unexpected intentional possibilities and thus worthy of discovery, that he cannot take them in hand as instruments for further development.

This fascination occurs because the animal lacks man's ability to withdraw from his own most fundamental, biological montages and to know them as "his." The human being can substitute one sense-structure achieved through these montages for another seen as equivalent; he perceives that both incarnate his presence in the world equally fully, although in different modes, instead of simply jumping like the animal from one field of action to the next, making no connections between one configuration and the next.

This superiority of human expression, the ability to count on past experience without becoming "stuck" in it as animals get stuck in their instincts, must originate in a capacity to pull out of the absolute present into, as Heidegger says, *noch nicht*—a "not yet"—from which the present can be viewed as present and the typical as typical. The human gesture uses the body's natural biological dispositions to express something more than this basic biological givenness: by his recul into the merely intended, man manages a projection in both directions and thus "on the spot," making of his own instruments a past to be used in extending command over the future. This paradoxical expression—a recul (backward) into the future (normally thought of as ahead)—is an attempt to render the miraculous nature of consciousness, of the originative moment in which time is ever newly founded and differentiated into its extases past and future. This phenomenon, which Merleau-Ponty describes in terms of "fission of Being," is the fulgurating, radiating power through which individuals exist, Being comes to be, and sense is born.

Two things should be noted about this sudden power of pulling clear, *échappement* (*PP*, p. 221), which manifests itself in the simplest intentional expressive comportment. First, it is not an indefinite, still less an infinite power of creation—of making anything out of anything. It is rather the renewed surge of energy of that which already exists, a possibility primitively given with the human corporeal montages themselves, so that its accomplishment is expansion, use, sublimation, or modulation of the materially given, functioning as possible instrument. Its achievement is thus in continuity with the "past," i.e. the primordially given which it modifies as its matter. Merleau-Ponty describes the creative gesture as a "backing up into the future" in order to remind us of this relationship between new and old. Similarly, when he speaks of the opening which allows a future to form itself in the present—consciousness itself—as *un vide déterminé,* not a néant, but a fold in Being, a formation of preexistent matter, he is reminding us of the contingency of man's creativity.

Second, the instant of advance, the *"voeu instantané,"* the "fulguration of thought" (*PP,* p. 213), requires the preceding given structures in order to incarnate itself, to gain endurance, and is therefore seen as a movement inhabiting them; the givens are in a sense the future's organs. This notion of organ is perhaps the happiest term Merleau-Ponty has found to express this relationship, for it avoids the impression which both matter and instrument can give of the higher moment impressing itself on the lower rather than inhabiting it as its own indispensable ground.

The gesture provides a particularly clear example of the paradoxical notion of a self-sufficient contingency, for as my body moves itself (*mon corps se meut*) in the gesture, I can easily perceive that it is both source and matter of the new sense it incarnates. But many of Merleau-Ponty's other images are less appropriate: for instance, the metaphor of thought directing language as the moon attracts the tides suggests a relationship altogether too external, for meaningful expression is more the cause than the effect of the corresponding *prise de conscience* of the universe. This consciousness itself, being but the animation of a structure already given, is a rebirth and extension of the former *sens* of its elements. The founded act is so firmly unified that one can say indifferently either that what comes to be—the new attitude—must incarnate itself in the power of the old dispositions or that what already exists must surge forward to take itself in hand.

In the painter at work, Merleau-Ponty found a graphic emblem of man's relative independence from his present in his particular modes of expression.[2] As he lays down his first line, two sets of motivation guide him: on the one hand, there is what he intends to picture and the demands of his medium; on the other, his style, which will make itself felt in both an individual and historical sense. His drawing will enter the history of art at a point that relates it to all that has already been accomplished by himself and all his predecessors. Matisse, for example, when looking at the woman he is about to draw, will adopt with his whole corps propre the stance of weathered painter and thus already sweep her up into his own styled world. His first line is then in a sense stylistically predetermined. Besides, it must respond to the exact need that impelled him to paint; it must structure a "coherent disequilibrium" which will be equivalent to the complex demands of the moment that challenged it into existence; within the norm of his style, it must echo the new modulation of Being that has called on the artist for expression. And finally, it itself will be determining, since as the first line is laid down, the entire field of the finished drawing will structure itself about it.

The line, explains "The Eye and the Spirit," is neither a thing nor an imitation of a thing, but rather "a certain disequilibrium provided (ménagé) in the indifference of the white paper, a certain forage pratiqué dans l'en soi, a certain constitutive emptiness, which emptiness, Moore's statues peremptorily show, is able to bear the pretended positivity of things. The line is no longer, as in classical geometry, the apparition of a being against an empty background; it is, as in modern geometrics, restriction, segregation, modulation of a pre-established [préalable] spatiality" (TM, p. 220), the general conditions of which have been laid down by the artist's corporeally grounded project. This spatiality on paper is the equivalent of the perceptual

2. We can never photograph the writer in the act, but the preservation of rejected sketches has something of the same revelatory power, achieving a breaking up of the necessary unity of the final expression, thus operating as a kind of reduction to make possible our discovery of the constitutive creative act.

world's, that aesthetic spatiality the corps propre normally projects and was projecting until the impact of the new experience provoked by the woman or Matisse's inspiration proved it inadequate. The resulting disequilibrium, demanding readjustment and restructuring is felt by the artist as a need for expression, and the first line of his drawing begins to incarnate and to answer that need.

This is true not only of the artist's lines—the ones he is in the process of laying down and all those he will eventually draw or has already drawn—but also, and for similar reasons, of the lines we first perceive in the natural spectacle. Such lines result from an attitude's living encounter with certain new givens which strike the individual, not as so many beings en soi, but as indications of planes, levels, and forces intruding themselves on a system of which he is conscious center. They express his effort to integrate these forces into the system he and they cohabit. Finally, the lines drawn by the act of perception also elicit the next developments in the perceiver's attitudes toward as well as within that system, just as each line Matisse lays down elicits his next creative stroke and, at the same time, focuses his conception of the final work.

Where then is the freedom, the creativity, of any new successful human expression? In a slow-motion film of Matisse during the creative act, the time of hesitation is dilated so that it is rendered solemn and given "the imminence of the beginning of the world." The brush which to the naked eye appears to leap from act to act can now be seen to hesitate as it meditatively attempts ten possible movements, dancing before the canvas (expression is a movement organizing a space!) and swiping at it two or three times, before it suddenly strikes it like lightning with the only necessary trace. Indeed, for Merleau-Ponty, here is the beginning of the world. But in what sense is the painter's action "necessary"? He is not the God of Leibniz, selecting from all possible alternatives the one and only best.

Matisse, installed in the time and in the vision of a man, looked at the open whole of his already-begun painting and brought the brush toward the trace which it called for so that the painting could finally be what it was in the process of becoming. . . . It is true that his hand hesitated, so there was a choice, and the chosen trace was selected because it fulfilled twenty conditions spread throughout the painting, unformulated, unformulatable by anyone else except Matisse, because they were defined and imposed only by his intention to make *this painting here which did not yet exist.* (*S,* pp. 57–58)

The reality of the created moment's vector—the power of the givens on the new order, of the matter on the form—is here made strikingly evident by the fact that the conditions consist not only of the precise nature of the need felt by Matisse—the still "unsaid" in what the woman has uncovered to him—but also of the response, the limitations, the demands of his material, the interaction of paper, lines, color, with the possibilities of equilibrium they suggest. This aspect of expression, so evident in painting that it overshadowed all the others for centuries, can be found in every other field of creativity, even those that at first sight seem "freest." It is present in the interaction of words and their attraction for and resistance to the author's thought and in the mutual effects of each man's intentions and desires and the political institutions of his society.

Every expression is a limited but creative act, the realization of a finite liberty. All poetic acts create by reference; their reality consists in the extension of an already given sense or, to put it slightly differently, in the crystallization of more sophisticated figures within the horizons (or against the ground) of a persisting world. Even the most creative artifact—if it proves successful—appears to "prolong the same furrow." The future, that void into which it is sucked, is determined, precluding any absolute surprises, because it is a "fold in Being," structured by all the sedimented experiences of the artist. It is a general-precise gamut of possible attitudes which, as the accumulated result of successful past encounters of a body with stimuli, are really powers of Being itself. The void that consciousness on the verge of expression opposes to the present fascinations of the world is not a *nichtigend Nichts,* but an ability to use generalized aspects of Being as instruments for creating a buffer against the powerful solicitations of the moment or, better, for striking a meaningful harmony among them.

Even the most primordial expression, the elementary gesture—

reaching to pick an apple, for instance—can be considered a way of "holding off the world." As I move to pick the apple, I "push to the horizons" the almost infinite range of potential radiations—solicitations—its presence in the world can have on me: I localize it precisely in relation to my biological body, so that the danger of its falling on me or my bumping into it accidentally is averted; it can no longer play the role of one splotch of living red among the hundreds on this tree; no surprise is left in its weight, distance, and shape; and the possibility of fulfilling my intentions in regard to it is no longer mere potentiality. Indeed, the only unknown left on this simple level of prise is my next reaction to its possession, but that will only become actualized in a new series of gestures. On a more complex level, in choosing (in the sense suggested above) to treat the apple only as a particular thing capable of satisfying my hunger, I have elected to pay no attention to its other relationships to the universe. I have thus ceased to interrogate it in all possible ways, which the *Phenomenology* indicates is the necessary condition of any "perception," any opposition of an object to a subject. By fixing it in only one of its possible senses, my configuration-instituting gesture pushes all the others into the undifferentiated opaqueness which makes of that Other "the thing," rather than merely a mode of my conscious self. And because I am able to live my gesture as only one possible mode of my existence, as a particular structuring of the moment that can nevertheless be related to innumerable other possible structures, I am content for the moment to conceive of those possibilities only as the thing's "substance"; I voluntarily leave that reservoir of possible discoveries untapped but comfortingly feel it to be accessible to any and all future efforts to make it explicit, provided only this thing retains its unity en soi. Collaterally, by virtue of its capacity not to become "stuck" in its own moment, the self itself is felt, in its opposition to the Other, as a dense reality which is also not exhausted in this prise. Hence the structure of the moment can be broken into from either side: a new meaningless brute disorganization can whirl in again or a new act of conscious attention can be solicited either by a sudden remorse on my part, motivating me to renounce the apple, or by the apple's falling suddenly from the tree just as I am reaching for it.

Such a momentary stance thus succeeds in "holding off the world" only for an instant, and it would be impossible to see in it the ground of any permanent hold on the world if it were unable to be retained in the corps propre in generalized form. The efficacy of my first gesture of reaching is not entirely expended when the apple is at last firmly in hand, for it then becomes one further step in the accumulation of a generalized power of distributing about me a familiar world of action whose noematic correlate is a whole universe of things I can unthinkingly handle. The body as living receptacle of savoir faire is ground of that orderly practical world of useful things (*Zuhandensein*) which is common sense's preferred domain. There, the whole system of accumulated equivalences I have been able to experience in moving from attitude to attitude is structured into a "world" of sense that is "lived" with a style I have developed.

The implications of Merleau-Ponty's remarks about gesture and art as illustrations of the essential aspects of expression extend to the very limits of his philosophical vision, and our understanding of them can perhaps be deepened by reweaving the tapestry of *Signs* strand by strand. But it is well to remember that, while *Signs* is intended to call us to experience for ourselves the phenomenon of expression in its many realms—in the institutions of social coexistence as well as language, in painting as well as exact science, in love as well as philosophy—it does not propose that the management of these forces can be reduced to a single formula, to an Idea of expressive power. Indeed, successful existence in one mode of expression does not assure success in all: the successful thinker is not necessarily also a good citizen and a great lover. No one can be taught to respect Being; each individual can acquire the art of properly using the forms of existence at his disposal only by first learning to recognize them for what they are and then reflecting on his own "living" of them within their proper field. Merleau-Ponty greatly feared that in some of the articles he himself had succumbed to the unpardonable sin of *la pensée de survol* (S, preface)—the erroneous mode of thought, both flight and assumption of independent superiority, that wills to abstract instead of incarnate. Actually, he might be accused of having avoided this danger almost too completely, for few philosophical writings of our time leave the task of abstraction and systematization so much to the reader, after he has first

responded to the invitation to rediscover for himself the experience
of expression.

Toward a Phenomenology of Language

We have now seen how the simple gesture typifies the more
complex and various forms of cultural expression. Language is undoubtedly the most complex system of expression, and the originative
word (*la parole parlante,* Heidegger's act of *anfängliche Denken*) is
itself a kind of expressive gesture: In the truly poetic moment that
incarnates a new point of view on things, it acts as a configuration-
forming corporeal attitude which helps us "hold off" the Other and
assert our stand in relation to it; like the other expressions of man's
finite freedom, it incarnates itself by using as its organ what is already
disposed in the *corps propre,* which it renovates creatively, thus
challenging further expression; the new word therefore takes place
"in the world," rather than appearing as an arbitrary epiphenomenon;
thus, once pronounced, it necessarily remains forever inserted in
time and is capable of sedimenting in its unique and remarkable way.

What then is so special about language? Why are we tempted to
think that it achieves the quintessence of what is human, exploiting
to the full the already staggering possibilities of human gesture?

The Word as Comportment

By "word" (*parole*) Merleau-Ponty does not mean the phonetic
unit (*mot*) but a self-contained meaningful expressive structure,
whether a single *mot* ("Fire!"), a whole poem, or an entire book. The
parole is one of those unified gestures in which a comportment comes
to grips with its environment, restructuring stimuli into a new configuration incarnating its own aims. In the originative word, what has
already been and what should come to be become one, and there is
achieved the "violent and mysterious passage from what I have to
what I aim at, from what I am to what I intend to be" (*PP,* p. 438).
The physical gesture is a modulation of our muscular body's grasp
on the world; it redisposes and restructures the whole perceptual

world—that "partial totality of Being"—about itself. Similarly the word is a modulation of our "phonematic body," of our language's grasp on the world; it also decenters and recenters the powers of language to make them express the "excess of what I am living over and beyond that which has already been said." The recentering of the world in both cases—the physical gesture and the verbal expression—because inscribed in "matter," whether perceptual or linguistic, is a social act. It can suck other behaviors into its wake; it alters their world materially; the first expression solicits further ones from them; it functions as a "furrow," an *aménagement de l'Etre* which they can espouse, imitate, *reprendre,* making it their own.

This is precisely what is demanded of a reader. The poor reader's mere mechanical repetition of the words is grotesque because he is handling the signs without grasping the sense of the gesture, without making it his own. The intelligent reader or conversationalist can commit a similar mistake when, meeting an expression foreign to his world, he says, "Oh, what you mean to say is," offers the appreciation, "Which really only comes down to," and follows that with one of the parodies of the original position that his world can allow. The authentic reader, by contrast, delivers himself up to the incantation of the word. He lets the author's style take hold of him, espousing its gesture, to form the proper configurations. As he moves with the rhythm, the style, adopting fully its point of view, he begins truly reading the sense that is between the words; he anticipates what the author wanted to say; he is now living that excess of the author's experience over what has already been said. Ultimately he may even feel justified in going beyond what is written to speak in the author's name: "What Descartes meant to say"; "What he would have answered in this case is." The reader can so completely possess the author's style —the unity woven by his project through the series of moments, the relation between figures within the major configuration (or *champ*) of the whole book and of that book to the entire *oeuvre*—that he comes to understand the original project itself, the *Urentwurf,* which in great literature and philosophy is the unity of the personality of the author himself. In short, he can comport himself as the author would. He lives in his world.

The Word Inhabits the Things

Words should not, however, be thought to have more to do with subjective attitudes than with things. Such a conception completely falsifies the fundamental reality of expression, for, just as there can be no things without a figure-forming attitude to bring them into being, so there can be no attitudes without the formation of figures which incarnate them. Since figures can be formed only by incarnating the intention in the matter of the body, the result will be "out there" not only for the subject but for all the other comportments which are in the world through participation in that same matter. A brief reconsideration of the role of the figure-forming attitude in even the simplest perception will clarify the sense in which "the words inhabit the things."

The task of perception is the discrimination and disposition of sensible stimuli into a manageable and intelligible *paysage* by means of patterns of recognition that the perceiver brings to the situation. Man confronts the especially complex problem of attending to constantly changing stimuli and integrating them into a continuous spectacle that makes sense for a unified consciousness; his orienting unification of the spectacle therefore has to be a dynamic process successfully anticipating and retaining stimuli. Ideally, for the spectacle to be absolutely true, to be fully comprehending and comprehensible by me and by all, rather than a fragmentary experience, the present configuration should be perfectly open and radiating, potentially correlating with all other possible configurations. All possible stimuli, and not only the stimuli of an instant ago or a moment from now, must always have been and must always remain accommodatable around the knot being held at the center of attention. The fullness of the humanly "lived" spectacle—the impression that present experience opens onto a world in which everything that is and can be must take place and in which everything finds its sense—is merely the all-encompassing anticipation of the possibility of such an integration relating every moment of existence and of duration to all others as various modalities of the present moment—modalities both of human perception and of thing as radiating center of innumerable possible points of view. Each thing is thus the intersection of a potentially infinite number of looks, of *regards,* a knot of countless strands of intention, meanings, and values. Such is the world-unifying task so remarkably performed by the schemes that interweave to form the human corps propre; this task is crowned by language and the thought it makes possible, for it is in language that this transition, this correlation between moments is carried out with the greatest plasticity, complexity, variety, precision, and, most mysterious of all, apparent transparency.

Once human perception is seen in the way just described, it is apparent that the schemes of the corps propre must be able to provide not just general world horizons (such as time, space, and the "categories"), but a more precise general "stuff." Kant recognized, in the famous passage on the Schemata, that the forms and categories, on one side, and sense stimuli, on the other, were not enough to account for our experience of things; somehow, through the mysterious activity of an "art hidden deep in the human soul," they must be brought together. It is to the description of this art, of this *Kunst,* that the aesthetic of Merleau-Ponty is devoted.

We should conceive the "stuff" stored in the body which that art, in the configuration-forming attitude, restructures when it composes the spectacle as essentially a cluster of equivalent trained powers (e.g. vision, movement, speech, etc.), as a kind of general memory (it would in this regard be interesting to trace Bergson's influence on Merleau-Ponty) of all the configurations ever adopted by those powers in the effort to structure the amorphous data offered them by their presence in the world. Whenever we seek to organize an experience into a retainable moment, the sedimented expressive attitudes of our various powers spontaneously enter into action reinforcing one another in motivating our new comportment. In the finished product of this synthesizing stance of the corps propre—in "the thing"— the new crystallization is so integrated with the stuff furnished by the corps propre out of the treasury of its experience as to make past experience indistinguishable from present data.

Of all our stored responses, the phonematic—because of their range, their abstraction, their flexibility—are the most important. They interweave with our muscular and nervous responses, with our sensations, to structure the thing. This is the sense of Merleau-Ponty's statement that things inhabit the words, and words the things. In so far as words have any content, it is, in Merleau-Ponty's own terms, an "emotional essence extracted" out of the things themselves. Reciprocally, the way things appear is influenced by the way the extracted essences—the ideas—guide the experience and direct the discourse of the perceiver. When I adopt a configuration-forming attitude, the resulting figure presents itself as a thing in the world; that world is the total lived unity of perception and idea, of the various "subworlds" corresponding to our various powers; this unity corresponds to the unity of the corps propre which integrates these subworlds as equivalent modalities of a continually unfolding panorama of things, persons, and their relations: my existence. In other words, the noematic correlative of the corps propre's integration of our various stored powers is the world, and within the world, the things. The various configurations that tie the moments of our experience together in any one of these modalities are always experienced as potentially livable in all the other modalities; the ideal total integration of the corresponding configurations from every modality into a single unit is what we mean by the thing, just as the ideal total integration of all things into a single unit is what we mean by the world. Every configuration is always lived, either as aspect of things or at least as referrable to things. Reciprocally, every configuration is experienced as in principle pronounceable, that is, each is felt in principle to have a possible expressive equivalent in the stuff of language. The general endeavor to incarnate the world in language is apprehended by us as coextensive with reality itself: whatever exists is presumed to be manageable in the world of linguistic discourse, just as it is presumed to be attainable in space or to be visible, given adequate instruments. The various subworlds, corresponding to our various powers—the linguistic, the kinetic, and the visual, for example—are "lived" by us as each *une partie totale du même Etre,* the world.

To illustrate this, let us consider the linguistic gesture's contribution to our structuring of the world, both in filling up and holding off things present and in achieving the pseudopresence of things absent. Nothing can make any clearer the extent to which the world of our physical experience is virtually indissociable from the world of language. These contributions can best be grasped by examination of the word's capacity to direct attention to unnoticed aspects of things; its imaginative-presentative power; its creative power as watchword [*mot d'ordre*] in politics or as new literary concept; and its capacity to let things be read between the words.

We saw earlier that a child differentiates colors more subtly as he comes to learn their names. At first he seems to recognize only dark and light, but after he has learned to avail himself of the sense incarnated in the words which crystallize others' previous accomplishments of finer chromatic articulations, he becomes able, taking those words up in his turn, to crystallize again the same articulations himself at will in the stuff of his own situation. The new structure, it should be noted, is experienced as in continuity with the structures that preceded it (the more recent chromatic formations are felt simply to preserve and deepen the truth of the earlier organization into gray and white). The source of this felt unity is what was noted earlier to distinguish human from animal comportment: the capacity to recognize the equivalence of every lived moment with every other. The new comportmental power caught by imitating the word is experienced by the child as moment of his own history. It finds its sense within his unfolding experience; it takes place within his horizons and so is one possible polarization of one world—his world. All the new steps in his growing linguistic ability are experiences of that world; what appear to him as configurations in language must appear to him as configurations in the world, as things, and his growing verbal command is an increasing ability to attend to those things as they are, to handle them by saying them. Whenever the human being finds he can express a thing, he feels that that thing had been lurking there in the perceptual world since the beginning of time just "waiting to be said," though he himself had never really experienced that thing fully in the visual mode until his linguistic expression of it.

Words are simply so many thing-structuring attitudes the individual has learned to take. But these attitudes are easier to handle than the kinetic or the visual; in their absence, things we want or seek can be commanded "magically" with greatest precision by reproducing in language the precise attitude equivalent to it. "To say that I imagine Pierre is to say that I procure the pseudopresence of Pierre by setting off the attitude 'Pierre.'" Merleau-Ponty explains further: "The function of the body in memory is that same function of projection we already encountered in the kinetic initiation [i.e. in reaching out for something or starting to move over to get it]: the body converts into vociferation a certain motor essence; unfolds in sound-phenomena the particular style of a word; deploys in a panorama of past experience the old attitude which I take up (*reprends*); projects in effective movement an intention of movement because it is a power of natural expression" (*PP*, p. 211). I can invite others to procure this pseudopresence verbally, precisely as I can invite them to attend to a particular present thing; indeed, I can virtually force it on them by pronouncing the word in their presence. When we are deep in conversation, we are attending to the words not as linguistic phenomena but as things or attitudes made present by our discourse, just as in the presence of actual stimuli, the center of attention is not my act of taking an attitude of kinetic initiation or of discoursing, exteriorly or interiorly (the same, essentially),[3] but is rather the thing crystallized by that attitude or discourse. Indeed, the thing is automatically filled out to such an extent that only the phenomenological attitude can ever reveal the fact of its constitution.

But the word's instrumentality in our hold on things is perhaps most clearly evident in the creative word, in the mot d'ordre. The politician who seeks to provoke a situation by expressing it calls social classes to self-consciousness and thus virtually brings them into existence as political forces, calling up revolutionary acts, designing new economic structures, and the like. Similarly, the best seller or the classic may provoke fads or unveil things previously unseen, creating such new modes of existence as the romantic *paysage,* the Oedipus Complex, the atom, the gene, the Will to Power.

Given all these considerations, we can go so far as to say that language is the very stuff of things if we keep in mind a distinction that Merleau-Ponty is not always careful to draw. (From the point of view of his basic position, it is not very important to him; but it will prove ultimately very revealing to us.) Neither as simple

3. "Ce silence prétendu est bruissant de paroles." *PP*, p. 213.

phonetic material nor as historical linguistic object can the word conjure up the full presence of a thing. It can achieve it only as corporeal stance, as attitude taken by the corps propre when it is pronounced. The true word does not stand for the attitude and does not merely accompany it in some way; it *is* that attitude. "Opening a new field or a new dimension of our existence" (*PP*, p. 213), it simultaneously accomplishes the bringing into being of a new dimension of things and (thus saving this creative fulguration from falling back into the néant out of which it comes) incarnates it in some kind of image. The verbal image is preferred simply because it is the most flexible and the most effective of all gestures. Hence, even from Merleau-Ponty's standpoint, it is perhaps somewhat misleading to declare that "the name is the essence of the object and resides in it in the same sense as (*au même titre que*) its color and its form" (*PP*, p. 207). If the term "name" is replaced by the phrase, "the dimension-opening and figure-forming attitude of the corps propre which incarnates itself in the word," the expression becomes exact, however, for it now indicates that, even when a word is pronounced, the corps propre need not offer the appropriate attitude (nor therefore the thing, in a real or in a pseudopresence), either because the full meaning of the word is not known to the speaker or because, as in the case of certain aphasias, the physiology of the corps propre cannot achieve its normal accomplishment.

The Peculiarities of Language

Up to this point, we have been considering the word as expressive gesture essentially like all the others. Let us now consider its particular advantages over all the other ways of taking hold of the world and holding it off.

Most expressive gestures function sufficiently when they make a thing present from only one angle. While the figure thus obtained is very partial, serving a rather narrow purpose for a definite span of time, the gesturer willingly renounces any attempt to control the other potential aspects of the thing left in obscurity, because the related intentions are not relevant to his present need in structuring the figure. This limitation of grasp to a narrow point of view in the behavior of higher animals incapable of language—for instance, the chimpanzee—can hardly be regarded as an option freely chosen in order to make possible a certain limited course of action. Köhler's report of the inability of his animals to solve certain problems which obviously they would have liked to solve, precisely because they were unable to vary points of view on the things involved, furnished by contrast the clue, in *The Structure of Behavior,* to the great range of power with which symbolic behavior equips the human being.

Language is the key to our power to vary points of view without losing hold of their equivalence; indeed, its very pretense of expressing not a point of view on things but things themselves is the summit and inevitable outcome of the fullest application of the symbolic power. "The essence of a thing," declares Merleau-Ponty, "is the presumption of a completed synthesis by which we have defined the thing" (*PP,* p. 445); the word that would say the thing itself pretends to have circumscribed the *noeud de relations,* the point of intersection where all the possible points of view come together, and to have grasped in itself that "stuff" of which the various points of view are only so many individual aspects. In this astonishing endeavor, a revolutionary transition is made from the modest motor gesture that seeks to grasp a thing from within a comfortable, limited angle, to the pretense of the ultimate expressive gesture that says what that thing is.

The word is an attempt to crystallize figures in a gesture so free of the point of view that solicited it and of the body that incarnated it that it can both express the situation in its generality—in other words, make present only that portion of it which is valid for all people and for all times—and be taken up by anybody in any situation from any point of view. A word is a gesture the sense of which all human comportments are able to grasp, because they enjoy the same body. When turning toward a particular radiating source of stimuli, any comportment can make the corresponding verbal gesture and form, from his point of view, an equivalent of figure. Moreover, as for example when procuring the pseudopresence of something not actually represented by any stimuli, I can always take up again a word previously pronounced and reproduce the same figure in a new situation within slightly different horizons, i.e. against a different fond, so that the thing named, although it appears at another moment in my experience, can be grasped as identical with the first but seen in a slightly different aspect. Thus the word is a gesture that makes it possible to multiply points of view on the same figure, projecting it against shifting fonds or turning about it as though it were a real center of radiation presenting an inexhaustible fund of constant stimuli. As long as I can hold that figure, that attitude, precisely—i.e. as long as I can continue to motivate the corps propre to form it—I (and other human comportments) shall be able to sediment in it all these new points of view. As the process can go to infinity and as very soon the *recoupements* of points of view will be so numerous as to be unrepresentable, concentrating rather as an opaque mass about the nucleus held precisely by the word, I tend to become unaware when using the word that I am still dealing with the figure from a point of view. Rather I consider it in its transcendence, taking for granted that, when saying the thing, I pronounce all the intentions that have gone and will go into it and presuming that the word, that "emotional essence" into which all of these experiences have been precipitated, could be analyzed to make explicit the various points of view that have gone and will go into producing it. When grasping the thing through the word, I usually take the emotional essence for the real essence, the presumption of a completed synthesis for an actual explication. The thing as held in the word then seems completely detachable from its material instruments (*PP*, p. 448), the idea from the word, the object from the verbal attitude that makes it present and fills it up and from the inevitably personal point of view which went into its production and vitiated its generality.

It is clear from this explanation that the word's peculiar power is simultaneously the source of its great effectiveness and the threat it poses. Within the limits of a familiar practical situation in which one seeks to carry out a modest material task, its familiarity, flexibility, and apparent transparency (meaning that it seems to refer directly to some "thing" that can be "handled," without itself having any importance as support for that sense) are great advantages. When I state firmly, "If Paul comes to work late again tomorrow, tell him I am not going to pay him for the whole day, as is only just," the things invoked surge up in the secretary's world as in mine and are grasped by the surface they present to both of us in this context. As long as our projects remain practical in this limited fashion, we can play the game; the thing can be communicated, the task dispatched, without our having inquired or even having been able to inquire very deeply into the nature of time, justice, or the true personality of Paul. But if all the things that come into the universe of my consideration are handled in this same way, when a situation arises which really calls for questioning into the sense of the things involved, there is real danger of my believing that because I can name them all I really know them in their essence; there is a risk that I will be satisfied with the familiar surface and never notice the relativity, the history, the various potential relations that radiate from the noeud. Indeed, since every word is in its depths tied not only to the whole world of language but to the entire experiential world, it is clear that if ever anything is to be said, if ever a moment is to be closed and action taken in the name of something—some "figure" crystallized— then a certain restriction of the whole, the acceptance of an "as if," is necessary. Language must, as all forms of action, partake in the inevitable metaphysical hypocrisy that gives all human acts their ambiguity.

If words were only objective signs, no sum or combination of individual words could ever make sense and sediment, allowing the individual to build a culture. But Truth is not an "I think": to believe that is to beget all the insoluble paradoxes of language and communication, to open the way inevitably to solipsism. Rather, Truth is an "I can": the capacity of the word to serve as a bridge between me and the others is based on the fact that language, of which this word is just one of the modifications, is itself one of my partial-total worlds of action, one sort of distributive general power that intercrosses with all the others to compose that world-opening power, my corps propre. Thus, as is the case for every expressive act, the configuration crystallized by the verbal act can only mean by recentering the whole world. Words have no sense in themselves, but rather mean only diacritically, by their interaction within the linguistic world. Hence the significance of Saussure's central discovery that signs convey meanings only by their similarity to and difference from other signs, by *recoupements* with one another; they "allude all together to a signification which, as long as they are considered one by one, is held off, and toward which signification I transcend without their ever actually containing it" (*S,* p. 110). This is the essential meaning of Merleau-Ponty's declarations that the sense germinates between the words rather than being contained in them; that every successful new pronouncement is woven out of *fils de silence* and stands out against a background of tacit intentions in just the way that the visible stands out against a *fond* of the invisible; that a classic is never so great as in the shadow it casts; and, finally, that the unfolding discourse has us more than we have it, since, although we struggle to direct its sense, it tends to unroll more and more with a vector of its own.

Hence no dictionary can exhaust a language's capacity to incarnate meaning; when learning a language, the best one can do is gather as many contexts as possible for each word and eventually allow these contexts to converge into the real meaning of the word. Once that converging has occurred, the person who can use a word would be hard pressed to express its meaning again except by referring back to the various contexts. As Montaigne said, I know better the sense of "man" than either that of "rational" or of "animal."

Hence also, in learning a language, I do not simply accumulate words—so many rather self-contained possible attitudes—any more than, in order to install myself in the World, I accumulate individual experiences of concrete things. Both of these misunderstandings overlook the meaning of "world" as a certain horizon into which I am fully installed with the first perception and interior to which all subsequent perceptions occur as further grasps of the same reality encountered in the initial grasp—as extensions, modulations, and finer articulations of what was formerly known. Similarly, when I am installed in a language—and this occurs the first time I am able to say something in it—I do not possess merely this or that word, but, rather, through the few expressions I can yet command, a whole way of "living" the world, a special system of powers takes hold of me and offers the world to me according to that language's characteristic style. This is why the best translations are produced when the writer himself attempts to live again in the second language the experience expressed in the first and why resorting to direct dictionary or grammatical equivalences leads to hopeless distortions. The phenomenon is very similar to that of sense of direction. I can move about my apartment distractedly; I do not have to take my bearings explicitly or consciously. As long as I do not think about it, the corps propre spontaneously makes available its whole "science" of space. Similarly, the sense language contains, its signifying power, is accumulated in it as a whole; when I start using it, it deploys itself spontaneously from the point of view of the words I am using just as the perceived world is spontaneously oriented from the point where I am now, and all the potential things not directly attended to are disposed invisibly and unconsciously about the configurations I have for the moment centered attentively before me. When I assume the attitude of a particular pronouncement, I invoke the whole linguistic world from that special angle. Even though that world is at first for me not very full, in crystallizing a phonematic figure, I reorder the entire linguistic world-fond in relation to it—or, rather, I must depend on the whole linguistic world to bear it up—and if I succeed in expressing something new, it is by decentering and recentering the whole language so that the excess of what I have lived over what has been said can incarnate itself. My statements are thus less actions I control than surges I set off. Hence, language tends more to possess me than I it, because it obviously always says infinitely more than I intend when I reorder the particular signs. In modeling the surface of language, I disturb it in its depths, and the whirlpool that I have set moving opens down into deeper waters than I realize, with the whole weight of the ocean disposing itself about it. Here again, the comparison with perception and movement is instructive, for perceiving, moving, and speaking are but modes of the same corporeal being-in-the-world. Whenever I attend to a figure or move to express my resulting stance out into the space of the world, my whole perspective on other things changes, and I begin to notice relations between the structures I brought to the center of attention and all the surrounding objects (including, on the margin, myself), which in turn force me to change my very conception of those structures themselves, my view of the background, and my understanding of myself as perceiver. Thus none of my intentions, once actuated, is ever quite what I originally planned it to be, and, at the same time, every one of my perceptions, every movement of my body in space, changes me as object and is perceived by others in a different way than I myself conceived it. In more ontological terms, the whole of Being must reorient itself according to the slightest displacement of that monadic point of view which I incarnate; indeed, it automatically does so because my corps propre is one with the system of the world, containing it implicitly even while it is contained by it. Likewise, when I say something new, I automatically not only use but also transform and enrich the whole language by forcing it to expand sufficiently to contain, to encompass, my new point of view. When I want to say something, what I hope to express is not out there before me—neither already preincarnated in language for me to repeat nor explicitly already possessed by me as clear and distinct idea, in a way that would make my pronouncing it, from my point of view, superfluous and therefore useful only to communicate my idea to others. In fact, my speech is intended to express as much for myself as for others, and I always learn in the process. As we saw earlier, whatever I want to say is first present in me as a dissatisfaction, as a need, as un vide déterminé, into which the available significations are sucked, dragging with them their whole reordering of the linguistic world and eliciting a sequence of further reprises. As a corollary, each of my creative pronouncements means more to others who interpret it than I intended to put into it; its silences themselves have meaning for them, and Husserl, for example, is as important for the unexploited fields he opens to our research as for the configured ideas he expressed.

LANGUAGE AS PECULIAR WORLD: CRITERIA FOR ITS TRUTH

All this being the case, Merleau-Ponty's incarnated view of language would appear to have an easy time with the old problem of the relationship between words and ideas. Once it is seen that the representation of things is the work of the corps propre and that the words are but the phonetic keys to the *clavier* of corporeal attitudes in which the things are phonematically sedimented and are thus themselves gestures that are, as such, inseparable from their own

sense (just as a movement cannot be reduced to equivalent photo-
graphic instants), then it becomes clear that form and content
(*la Forme et le Fond*) cannot be rigorously separated. Since ideas
cannot be without the words, language and the recuperation of truth
are one. A corollary victory seems to have been achieved over the
old aporias about universals by the careful establishment of the
generality of the corps propre's activity.

But Merleau-Ponty has in fact simply displaced the content-form
problem by restating it in a new and hence particularly difficult form.
Thought is for him so incarnated in language that the difficulty now
becomes one of understanding how thought and language can ever
anchor at all in any reality other than themselves, how they will
ever encounter any limit to their free interplay. The only available
criterion of validity seems to be a certain internal coherence of sense:
can one talk of an idea's truth or falseness so long as it manages to
incarnate its author's intention, any more than one can talk of a
gesture's being true or false? The theory's tendency to lock language
in on itself is aided and abetted by our undeniable experience that
language does tend to "run away with itself" and thus to serve as the
field par excellence of activism (in the sense discussed at the beginning
of this chapter). Language's peculiar way of accumulating a sense
results in the illusion of transparency which invites ideas to deny their
own limits—to take themselves for absolute adequation of the things
themselves—thus encouraging action to slip its proper anchors in
the situation.

Because language would speak of all the other partial-total worlds,
it is obvious that the problem of the criterion for the truth of a word
is especially critical. Given Merleau-Ponty's ontology, however, the
problem of activism must also plague the other higher forms of
expression. Serious consideration of painting or politics does indeed
lead eventually to the same question, but each presents the dilemma
in its own way; in his last essays, Merleau-Ponty can therefore play
the various forms of higher expression off against each other in an
effort to illumine the human situation as such and the possibilities
it offers for meaningful existence.

The ontological nature of the problem confronting the human
existent can be couched in the simplest of general terms: if man is

that comportment which achieves the highest manifestation of Being (that is to say, if the *Dasein* is he who can open a space, *aménager* planes, profiles, hollows, and crests so that Being can contemplate itself), then his fulfillment lies in the achievement of as full and rich a self-possession of Being as possible. What this practically entails, however, is a more complicated question. The distinguishing of moments, which, as Plotinus already saw, is the sine qua non for Being's reflection on itself, is achieved by pushing back the totality of what is to the horizons, causing it to serve as fond against which a distinctive figure can outline itself as object of the individual consciousness. That consciousness, as summit of Being, alone can contemplate the figure and, through it, its fond—Being itself. As it is the very center of the process which allows Being to be—to contemplate itself through a finite consciousness—that consciousness naturally tends to take itself, and especially its production, for reality itself, allowing the figure to blind the perceiver to the fond which it is the figure's main purpose to "reveal as invisible," allowing the moment to hide its dependency on the whole of the history which supports it and which it supports. This failure to relate itself to the whole, to recognize the moment as intersection of innumerable planes of Being, is the error which can disqualify a statement. It is the source of non-sense in the strictest meaning of the term, for the essence of "sense" is the capacity to relate moments in a dynamic way so that consciousness can grasp them as simultaneously radiating out to the whole of "brute Being." As we saw earlier, only comportments signify, for they relate centers of radiation not only as compossible but as coexistent, dynamic moments harmonized both temporally and spatially. Waking comportments signify—achieving intentional transgressions—because they can relate one order of facts to another, while dreams do not because they abandon themselves to a single mode of existence—sexuality, for instance—without full reference to the physical world.

However, given that no statement, no moments, no figure can by nature ever make full sense, ever make completely explicit all that it implies, hiding at the same time that it reveals, its hiding and revealing must certainly be a matter of degree. The activistic is thus separated from the fruitful-suggestive moment by a difference which, however important, is only one of degree. By gathering together suggestions scattered throughout Merleau-Ponty's last essays, we can see some of the ways in which the various forms of expression, each kind of figure-forming, can be activistic. This will help us to understand why language of its very nature tends to activism more than the other forms and to see the ways in which literature and philosophy should confront this problem.

Music would seem to be the one exception, an art which of its nature is not tempted to activism. It is "too much this side of (*en deçà de*) the world and the designatable to figure anything other than bare diagrams of Being (*épures de l'Etre*), its flux and its reflux, its surge, its eruptions, its whirlings" (*TM*, p. 195). Music presents no figure circumscribable enough to set itself up as an apparently adequate end of action en soi, no thing in which one can install one's projects, enjoying the illusion of comprehending what is. But exactly to the extent that it remains so shapeless it will fail to bring much to consciousness as it lulls one back into fascination, its characteristic sort of failure.

Painting, by contrast, can and does make present the world in crystallizations, even going as far as attempting to reproduce things as they are. Inauthentic painting par excellence is that which, in devotion to a cause (or perhaps only to a superficial idea, such as that of practical common sense, about the nature of things), believes it has found the ultimate formula for capturing any aspect of the world's spectacle and rendering it fully on canvas. This error is not inevitable: the great painter was never at any time a mere camera eye, and even commonsense criticism has always demanded that his work be true not to the retina, but to life. Authentic painting always recognizes and meets the ontological problem of configuration, even when unconscious of its philosophical implications, for the painter has to grasp the things he meets in a four-dimensional perceptual experience and then distribute the four dimensions on his two-dimensional canvas. Thus, no matter what his convictions about the reality of the things he sees and about their relation to what he has painted, he is aware that he must resort to artificial methods of representation to present and structure his vision of the world. He voluntarily adopts systems of equivalence as modes of world- and self-expression; his criterion of any such system's success is whether or not he and others can recognize the resulting configurations as true to their experience of a world where things, each of which asserts itself as a center of Being, become compossible as they are synchronized in the visual act. The particular system of equivalences chosen by the painter is clearly not what determines this success. Renaissance perspectives, impressionistic color values, or cubist volumes are not in themselves panaceas or definitive solutions, any more than they can ever be considered errors per se. Ultimately, what each technique suggests can never be fully expressed, for it implies the knotting of numerous planes of Being, each a partial-total world of its own, into a momentary configuration of the painter's world. Hence they are merely modes of questioning things and their coexistence, modes of suggesting the internal movement by which things become compossible in vision. The only advantage that modern abstract painting has over traditional representational approach is that, by "multiplying systems of equivalences" (*TM*, p. 218) —depth, space, line, color, motion, words, materials of all kinds— it has broken once and for all the adherence of painting to the surface of things. Even the superficial amateur has been forced to recognize that the real end of a painting, as all great artists have always known, is to discover, to uncover our visual world in the making. A painter must help others experience the reality of the life of things, of that which is not his or the viewer's ego; he must force the contemplator to go out of himself in order to assist (*assister* meaning both to be present, looking on, and to help) at the "fission of Being, only at the end of which [process], I close on myself" (*TM*, p. 222).

This last statement is difficult and vitally important. The end of a painting, indeed, the ultimate, authentic end of any configuration, is not to permit me to have the thing, but to open me to a possession that is bipolar, often described by Merleau-Ponty in terms of "magic." Painting aims at re-creating the intentional transgression that is the source of all sense—that moment where I first grasped the world as other; it aims at provoking the movement of pulling back into the "not-yet" in order to allow the infinitely suggestive power of the brute "what-is" to reveal itself, thus permitting each frozen structured thing to suggest its invisible sides, its own partial-total world.

These considerations are necessary for proper interpretation of those texts in *"L'Œil et l'esprit"* which declare that "all flesh, and even that of the world, radiates outside itself" so that "the God of things [is] the Sun" (*TM*, p. 223) and that the painter seeks to render the internal animation of things, to show them as *déflagrations de l'Etre,* to bring out their preexistence. Clearly, Merleau-Ponty is not abandoning here the transcendental point of view and suggesting a world other than that we can constitute; rather, he is simply affirming the potentially endless capacity of our world to expand through our every effort to get unstuck from what we already possess, that is, to improve it. This *rayonnement* of things (i.e. of the world we meet as given, as already figured) is but the constituting power of everything which has a *manière d'être* (*TM*, p. 219), the capacity of every already structured object to serve as dimension—to suggest beyond itself, to remind us of the simultaneity of all our instants of experience in the unity of silent Being. As a necessary corollary, it must not be overlooked that, for things to radiate signification, we must "lend our body to Being"; it is the corps propre which must compute the interaction between what is already figured and what will be. "One can be spectacle of things only by being spectacle of no thing" (that is, by getting stuck in no one figure); only in this way can one achieve the epitome of human contemplation, which consists in showing how "the things make themselves thing, and the world, world"— Merleau-Ponty's most extreme Heideggerism—*die Welt weltet!* (*TM*, p. 217).

In sum, the painter's aim is to make the contemplator aware of the miracle of creativity which is hidden in his own perceptive act, in even the most modest prereflexive advance beyond the bare givens. The painter who fails to make us see that our perception opens us onto a fathomless sea of reality, ever capable of deepening and reformulating, is activistic in that, by setting a definite goal to his activity, he distorts its true nature, which is to make other activity in its turn possible. Activism paradoxically limits the dynamic power of the gesture to the definite accomplishment of *this* figure which in itself and for itself ultimately signifies, structures, indeed figures, nothing. Without the reference beyond, without the revelation of the *transgression intentionelle,* the figure that would be in and for itself hides the unlimited fecundity of each present (*fécondité illimitée de chaque présent*) and is therefore not true, is non-sense.

Since painting is anchored in the direct meeting with the world through perception, it cannot be tempted to hide the opacity of the moment the artist seeks to represent. We perceive Nature, things, directly as foreign and as imperfectly grasped because the act of perception is always felt to be capable of further extension, of better and closer focus, for instance. Any perception is thus experienced directly as moment of an accumulative and protensive process. The very effort to grasp that moment and reproduce it as one possible hold on the Other, however, involves the danger of separating from the process its partial product, so that it can be contemplated and given a kind of eternalized validity. Satisfaction with the "instantized" equivalent thus obtained, independent of the living reality to which it refers and in which alone it has its deep sense, fails to realize the role of the existent as bridge between moments, as support for opacity, as source of the inexhaustibility and dynamic sense of every partial-total world.

Literature that presents facts, hiding the contingency of the whole system in which alone they have any interest or any sense, fails in the same way: the success of the system of equivalences hides the system as a moment unifying moments, as a point of view whose value is to open horizons rather than to contain its object. A literature in which the reader becomes stuck in eroticism or fascinated by the plot or converted to a thesis; a science that begins to believe absolutely in its concepts; a philosophy that can no longer see the limits and the dependence of its Weltanschauung—all of these err because they have followed the natural inclination of the self-conscious moment to become an end in itself, to assert itself as noncontingent and "all there," as fully self-captured. The same is true of the politique which loses the sense of the limits of its slogans, so that "capitalist imperialists," "*mir y drushba*," or "free enterprise" become entities existing absolutely en soi, as self-sufficient truths independent of the system, which system itself becomes grasped as independent sum of these truths rather than as what it is in fact, only a way of viewing the situation and of seeking to handle it.

Music tends to lull us into fascinated joy in pure, formless dyna-

mism; painting threatens to freeze us into contemplation of a moment
artificially snatched out of the life stream. Yet they have a salutary
counterbalancing effect on the person possessed by language. For
language does more than arrest moments in which I somehow manage
to structure my direct experience of the world. It also attempts to
relate those moments to all other similar ones, whether my own or
other people's, by inserting them in a system of signs transmittable
from one existent to the next. The word asserts itself as "capable
in principle of capturing any Being that may present itself" (S,
p. 119); the figuration is grasped not merely as a finished product,
valid independent of the existence that had once secreted it, but as
objectively valid per se; it is no longer recognized as a product at
all but, rather, as a reality existing in and for itself from all times
and for all times. The activistic temptation of language lies in the
tendency to believe that it has been able not just to extract an eternal
presence from the flux of time, but to condense the flux of time
itself, to possess its sense absolutely in a truth that is independent
of any act that would have to produce it. This illusion is given
credence by the indisputable fact that every new significative intention mutely felt as truth to be expressed must, in order to incarnate
itself at all, be able "to incorporate itself into culture—mine and the
other's as well—to mold me and to mold him by transforming the
sense of the cultural instruments" (S, p. 117). I must really be able
to center and recenter the whole of language in order to express that
excess of what I live over what has already been said. Consequently,
the authentic word—the new philosophy, the horizon-opening novel,
the great and productive politique—cannot help confronting bravely
its time and facing its historical situation. It must aim at commanding
and bringing to a head the whole destiny of the language, at revealing
"what it has always awaited to say"; it must relate itself to and
challenge all other men's truths, assert itself as fuller enunciation of
that toward which men of the past were groping, and demand that
all future developments take it explicitly into account, that less adequate points of view among contemporaries conform themselves to it
(in the sense that the great classic creates its own audience). No
wonder then that the creative word should tend to take itself as a
final solution: having subsumed into its more adequate formulation

the sense of what all its predecessors wanted to say, even while it remains perfectly self-possessed, it comes to regard itself (as in the paradigm of Hegel) as that which really crowns, commands, and recaptures, once and for all, the sense of history.

Again, this is both a weakness and a force, as a contrast of the greatest literature with the most authentic painting will make clear. The painter is not tempted to think that he can positively subsume the whole truth of the tradition of painting into his canvas or that he can be the voice of his time. Indeed, the opacity of his medium encourages him to accept completely his existence as a solitary, inhabited, interiorized moment, one valid synthesis of points of view. As a sense-giving individual, he can carry out a successful recuperation by means of an organizing gesture; and thus an opportunity to be at the service of Being is opened for him. Though superficially (and only apparently) the opacity severs him from the flow of history, it also anchors him more securely in the particular instant. He is cut off from any conscious intersubjective dialogue, but he is also invested in the brute, precultural, fundamental dialogue of our perceptual presence to the world, that most primordial of intentional transgressions. The centering of his attention on his own gesture—both his perceptual gesture and its extension and reprise in the pictorial—reveals it as momentary, limited, contingent; it is almost impersonal, for it originates in a call of and is reinvested in matter, but he can nevertheless assert it as meaningful, as sense-giving.

The attractiveness of contemporary painting, as we mentioned previously, lies in its peculiar capacity to call attention to its system of equivalences precisely as gestures, manifesting clearly their insufficiency as well as their inevitability. It suggests the mysterious, necessary relation of the gestures to a truth that they never can say but only can imply by asserting themselves as deformations of it, albeit coherent and thus meaningful deformations (S, p. 68). The very strangeness, the satisfied individuality, the opacity, indeed the inaccessibility of modern painting emphasizes more than ever before in the history of art the need for each man perpetually to structure and restructure the givens of the moment. The viewer, like the painter, must accept the individualism, the limits, and the contingency of the momentary gesture as inevitably linked to the very nature of sense, to the necessity for man to reveal Being only in series of partial truths. The difficulty here, of course, is that partial truths can be truths only by being also in some way total—that is, by asserting themselves not only as moments but as moments of something that in some way embraces all that is.

The very limits of painting, which prevent its even pretending to totality, do, of course, save it from the dangers of language's metaphysical hypocrisy—the pretension of "extracting the sense out of the signs, of isolating it in its pure state" (S, p. 95). The philosophy or science that thinks it has attained totality ignores the extent to which its own medium still "gets in the way" and is inseparable from its version of the truth. Its style, silences, and oversights are as expressive as its most explicit statements. The painter would never dream of "separating the sense of the work from its configuration" (S, p. 96) or of considering his produced configuration merely a technical instrument at the service of an exterior end. But he is truly limited however and, in his turn, may be lured to the opposite form of hypocrisy: to reduce the sense to the configuration as he founds the meaning of his work in what Merleau-Ponty terms an *éternité hypocrite* (S, p. 99). When he believes the configuration to contain the sense—simply to be meaningful once and for all, without having to point at or depend on anything beyond itself—he properly does not look upon it as a mere tool, but he misconceives it as an end in itself. Thus he hypocritically ignores the very tradition which alone can give his work its perpetual value. In wanting his masterpiece to rest in itself, he would hide the fact that, to have any sense at all, it needs to be taken up, relived, re-created in some way by men; this is all too easy to forget, for, unlike language, painting makes no explicit reference to the unconscious dialogue with all previous and future painting and all previous and future perceiving upon which it depends.

Ironically, painting's flight into a supposedly eternal present prevents it from confronting its real present. Incapable of the writer's direct dialogue with his predecessors and explicit challenge to his contemporaries, the painter is restricted to vague evocations of his time; touched with a bit of the antiquarian, he cannot bravely confront the époque. In their attempt to re-create perfectly the living reality, his configurations do manage to recognize one sort of thickness and irreducible opacity, spatial opacity, that of "thingness," but at the same time they are blind to another, the opacity and reality of historicity. As a result, historicity marks the plastic arts more than it is marked by them. The Apollo of Olympia, huge and majestic, solid and imposing as it is, seems a fragment eroded by time, wrapped in the aura of an unattainable past, whose sense can be fully recognized no longer. In contrast, the scattered bits of Anaximander's text keep alive his eternally valid questions, challenging us with a very precise momentary vision. His whole situation is pulled into our present because to comprehend the text we must adjust our own vision to his; thus it manages to have a clear sense for us, a contemporary relevance that the sculptural remains of Aegina can never have.

Between these extremes—concrete art with its configurations, on the one hand, and abstract thought with its sense, on the other— literature would seem to offer the possibility of some compromise. The successful literary author should be protected from both sorts of activism by recognizing the necessity for both form and fond, thesis and style, sense and configuration in his work. The novel, for example, asserts itself as a point of view to be embraced by the reader, to be sure, but that point of view is intended to reveal the truth of the life it describes and thus to challenge all other points of view to enter into dialogue with it. Even while it recognizes its incapacity to express fully its perspective and thus leans on its style to direct the reader to the work's real center, the novel uses this perspective on things "to inaugurate discussion, to suscitate research" (S, p. 96) rather than merely to provoke mute contemplation. As not merely a point of view, but a point of view on points of view,[4] the novel does invest itself in opaque facts and things, but in a way that forces them to reveal their synchronization by referring them constantly to the unifying, underlying movement, source, and sense of the surface crystallizations—the unity of the animating fundamental project, the *Urentwurf,* which ties all the various moments of the work into the unity of a style and proposes the work specifically as a partial-

4. Merleau-Ponty's admiration for Proust here receives its explicit ontological foundation. The study on the Sartre–Nizan dialogue in the preface to *Signs* is itself revealing in regard to this question of "points of view."

total, not as an absolute truth, as a meaningful possible variation of man's basic insertion, through expression, into the world.

This very position, however, also exposes literature to the temptations of both painting and language, as the *pièce à thèse,* on the one hand, and the formalistic work, on the other, clearly illustrate. Literary criticism will remain torn between advocates of art for art's sake and those of a *littérature engagée* until a theory of style is developed that is capable of "setting the word above technique or instrumentality and recovering it in its essence" (*S,* p. 96). It must be made clear that the value of a word is not limited to what it says: indeed, its *vérité logique,* its *signification d'énoncé* offers access not to any one object of thought, but to him who thinks, to his "native cohesion," of which "the being of things and that of ideas are but replicas." An adequate theory of style would reinsert the word into its full cultural context without losing its originality. This is what it means to grasp the concept as a configuration having a sense because it successfully polarizes anew the whole of Being evoked as its fond: the concept is "opened without being destroyed." This immense task, this unending endeavor of reconciliation of the opaque and the transparent is the authentic challenge of philosophy itself.

Philosophy then not only crowns but saves all the other enterprises of human expression. The philosopher would fulfill the original *voeu* of culture itself, which is already latent in the primordial faith that made human perception human and which is brought to full consciousness in language; this is *le voeu d'une recupération totale du monde,* the effort to have all experience make sense. Animal behavior succeeds in achieving a kind of instantaneous sense by organizing momentary *champs d'action* but exhausts itself by producing kaleidoscopically ever-new, unrelated fields as the situation changes, while the human gesture manages to conquer and extend this sense, bridging moments and founding the meaning of each existent in the affective unity of a life in which each field is grasped as substitution of one equivalent structure for another. The cultural development "spreads beyond the limits of one individual's life the same kind of envelopment which links and unifies in advance, from the instant of birth, all the moments of that life. The signification of the work of art lies in the part it plays in the life of culture, in the historical process within which it is founded in signification" (*S*, p. 86). Philosophy crowns the process of culture by bringing the whole of it to explicit consciousness, rendering to the individual gesture the maximum of sense by placing it in a context that extends infinitely before, around, and after it; in this way it secures perpetual meaning for the gesture, while reasserting the validity of culture as the fond and flesh of the coherent configuration. In bringing to light the "triple reprise" which gives the individual expressive act that *éternité provisoire*—that is to say, its anchor in what already is (the things, the expressive agent's own past, and his models in the tradition)—philosophy is not just devoted to history but is the future-opening enterprise itself. Its illumination of roots in the past in a way that respects Being inevitably opens inexhaustible fields of future inquiry.

Philosophy then is the effort to grasp one's own configurations as configurations, to see them in their fullest context, to find their place in the tradition, and to return to the cohesion of the original instant, the moment in which the existent tore himself from his givens to dominate them and to extend their sense. To learn more precisely philosophy's program, we must turn more to what Merleau-Ponty has done than to what he has said about philosophizing. The philosopher alone, he tells us, is free enough to achieve the ultimate hermeneutic task; the philosophical attitude alone liberates the reflective activity of man from the need "to play the game of passion, of life, of the imaginary," by choosing as its own the supreme goal, "precisely that of unveiling the Being we inhabit." Like the Ego itself, philosophy is then without any specific instruments or organs (*S*, p. 20) and thus can inhabit freely all the instruments at hand, giving them a voice and a sense without itself having to adhere to any of them. This should not, however, be mistaken for a freedom of survol—of disinterested surveillance; again, like that of the Ego, it is a freedom to engage. A soul is nothing without a body to animate, and a philosophy is nothing without configurations to relate to one another. Just as the personal Ego stands atop the pyramid of his past, philosophy stands atop the mammoth pyramid formed by the whole of culture in order to give it its full sense.

Merleau-Ponty's essays on art, history, psychology, sociology, and

science all have expressly one end in view: to discover under the
surface of particular configurations the unifying factor that he terms
their texture, their logic, their structure, their proper virtue, their
symbolics, or, perhaps best of all, *le fondamental*. (The last term
refers most clearly to Heidegger's *existentiale*, which is not just the
structure of the *Dasein* himself, but the *Dasein's* structuring of the
Being that comes to be in the *Geschehen*). Philosophizing is seeking
"the *syntax* of gesture, the *order* of culture and sense, of the *avènement*
[the Advent]" which founds each expressive act in truth (*S*, p. 200)
—in short, a *typique* of the *atypique*.

Given that the syntax is modified by each new configuration, the
endlessness of the quest and indeed its paradoxical nature should be
apparent. Being is nothing but the coherent whole of which each
figure reveals a facet, a dimension, a focus; and thus if, as Heidegger
put it, *das Sein nie west ohne die Seienden,* it is clear that each new
figure, including even that achieved by the philosopher's recovery,
opens new horizons, offers the challenge of further recuperation.
Merleau-Ponty's conception of philosophy is in no sense an answer
but an unending program of inquiry. He offers no substitute for
patient and respectful dialogue with the classics, no shortcut to a
direct grasp of Being. There is no other access to Being than the
continuing effort to insinuate oneself into those indispensable moments of vision which have stamped the sense of all that followed.

RECUPERATION OF THE WORLD AND
THE CLASSICAL FIGURES

Merleau-Ponty may seem to be proposing a Hegelian synthesis
of past positions into a global prise de conscience which would constitute the ultimate triumph of Spirit; but his very explicit denega-
tions of this conclusion reveal an important aspect of his conception
of the very status of the individual figure. Hegel or the philosopher
who follows him may be able to subsume (*aufheben*) the classical
positions, those *pensées en deça desquelles on ne revient pas* (*S*,
p. 193), insofar as they are positive assertions—in other words, to the
extent that they lead directly to his present position—but he neglects
the very essential meaning that lies in what they deny or in what

they leave unsaid (*ce fond de silence qui envelope tout ce qui est dit*). The sense of Descartes' philosophy, for instance, is enclosed not in the figures he developed—the Cogito, the project of construction of space, and the like—but in the invisible they hide and, in hiding, suggest. The truth of those figures lies both in their struggle with expressions that preceded them and against which they were affirmed (e.g. the attempt to conceive of space ideally is valid when it is seen to oppose a hidden empiricism but becomes false if Descartes' construction is taken to be true in itself, just as a revolutionary program loses its validity when it hardens into a régime) and also in the struggles they themselves unleash (not in the Cartesians' almost rote repetition of the Cogito as a formula, but in all the developments the Cartesian constructions have subsequently provoked, especially that final conquering of the subjective viewpoint which makes Cartesianism a "point of no return").

This is not to suggest, however, that the great philosophies have no sense properly in themselves, for the very fruitfulness of the long dialogue Merleau-Ponty himself has carried out with Cartesianism proves the contrary. It is clear that Merleau-Ponty's "effort to return to the fundamental and the spontaneous source of all thought," to understand the nature of our freedom, would be unthinkable without the impetus provided by the Cartesian dilemma. But such fruits can be obtained only from intercourse with the classical (or any other) position if, armed with what we know of what preceded and what followed it, we try to slide back into its point of view, to situate ourselves in it as fully as possible, in order to witness from the inside, *comprendre de l'intérieur* (S, p. 225), its work at structuring Being, in much the way that the painter seeks "to assist at the fission of Being." We then see not merely another typical example of configuration forming to bring about one more revelation of Being, not even another step in the construction of the horizons within which we now live (which can indeed be witnessed in any and every configurating act), but rather the significant transmutation, carried out by each great classic, "of its situation of origin into a means for comprehending itself and for comprehending others" (S, p. 163). Once a philosopher has contemplated space, to take one example, from the unique angle presented in Descartes' *Optics*, where it is unlike space as it appears in any other work, this concept can continually throw light on all preceding or following philosophy, as Merleau-Ponty has proven by returning to the *Optics* again and again, until the very end, where *"L'Œil et l'esprit"* is once again a commentary on it. Since each important historical moment is valuable because it manages to open onto "the whole world at that time," its independence can never be legitimately alienated (any more than another Ego encountered in perception can be absorbed by the perceiver). Rather, such moments can be related to me only as "circuits within my circuit"; each must be related to all others as well as to mine, and the whole interpenetrating exchange of anticipations and significations which is history's secret life must be allowed to subsist among all these equivalent and simultaneous "open significations" (*S*, p. 103).

This effort to encompass our history is obviously an almost vertiginous enterprise. It is of course possible to "live" any world subconsciously, without questioning one's true relationship to it. But precisely to the degree that one does live in this manner, he is trapped in the eternal Oedipus cycle which plagues all culture unreflectively received—the rejection, omission, or destruction of what in truth founds it, a self-ignorance which keeps the existent functioning in this way from knowing the true potential of his creative acts, which may en soi be fruitful and creative but pour soi can never really find their sense. While the painter may find this situation acceptable, though painful, the philosophical gesture, the human act par excellence, cannot, as its very essence is the attempt to possess its own sense. As we have seen, the particular quality of human nature is not its possession of some original equipment that other animals do not enjoy but simply its ability to arrive at moments when "a life woven of chance turns back on itself, takes hold of itself, expresses itself" (*S*, p. 305). Such moments are always miracles, and in the fact that their universalization has been dared at all can be found the very superiority of our tradition: "It is a matter of fact that there has occurred such a miraculous turning back of a historical structure on itself: through it, Occidental thought has emerged from its particularity and its 'locality.' Thus were founded a presumption, an intention which still await their accomplishment" (*S*, p. 173). The philosopher, cariatide du vide, human being par excellence, makes the tradition live by accepting the challenge of truth, the task of making the sacred be. He can turn to no ready-made truth, no *Heilige* in itself, waiting passively for his discovery; rather, the enterprise of spontaneous interaction, of recoupement, of reciprocal confirmation of many lives awaits him potentially in art, in literature, in politics, perhaps even in philosophy. The philosopher must search for it *partout*—everywhere—and must not believe he has found it *nulle part*—anywhere. The logic of Being is found *nulle part et partout* "wherever there is manifest a human rapport with the world, a revelation of Being"; in every one of them and in all of them it can be discovered, as the fundamental of co-presence, that *"jointure et membrure de l'Etre qui s'accomplit à travers l'homme."*

If Merleau-Ponty's theory must be summed up in one word, that word is "humanism" in the sense just described. His method is the call for what Heidegger rightly terms a hermeneutic that can bring out the sense of all the figures and is thus, in the most profound sense of the term, an aesthetic. If a master for his effort should be designated, even more significant than the great Germans who so readily come to mind—the last summits of transcendental philosophy, Husserl and Heidegger—are the names in the tradition of modern French humanism: Mallarmé, Valéry, Bergson, Proust. Had it not been for the poignant little essay in *Signs,* however, so obviously an intellectual autobiography, his ultimate master might have been overlooked, for he is a contemporary only in the eternal sense. Michel de Montaigne is present in the last essays almost as a kind of answer to the difficulty that inevitably obsesses their reader: Can such a vertiginous enterprise really be lived? Montaigne haunts *Signs* as though to say that it can because I did and thereby won the only true immortality available to the cariatide du vide.

CHAPTER 6

Toward the Rehabilitation of Reason

THE DIFFICULTIES that make themselves felt with rising tension in the last essays are not due to some hidden error in logic, nor are they the revenge of an order of facts overlooked. Rather, they are manifestations of the central problems present in the transcendental viewpoint itself. But the transcendental viewpoint has imposed itself progressively on Western civilization since the Renaissance—and now, through the occidentalization of the rest of the world, upon all men—and it may therefore be affirmed that the difficulties developing in Merleau-Ponty's philosophy are rooted deeply enough to reveal something of the human condition itself. We are dealing with that rare phenomenon, an authentic philosophy.

The transcendental viewpoint, once matured, envisions the overcoming of the traditional inauthentic subject-object separation and thus of the banal forms of all empiricism-idealism aporias. Having recognized that Being is encountered only within human experience, the transcendental philosopher probes the ultimate horizons of that experience, seeking to grasp the englobing sense of what appears within them. For him, no one moment of experience can pretend to absoluteness, for all moments depend on and ultimately refer to what is left implicit in those horizons. With this realization, the problem of the One and the Many receives its ultimate formulation. And as this point of view comes into full possession of itself, its own early division is resolved: the *Ding-an-sich,* or brute Being, no longer carries on a ghostly existence beyond the horizons of experience but, rather, because it is those horizons, it is recognized as an essential element of all phenomena, as their very texture. It is shown to be present in all projects as that drag—the adversité, the inertia of the fond—revealed by the configurating moment. It is that against which each creative act must prevail to open a future while depending on it—the irreducible otherness which founds every Ego and every moment of Ego, the *profondeur* of every thing, the unending eloquence of every quality. The aporias of all the subject-object formulations are thus replaced in Merleau-Ponty's philosophy, as they already had been in Hegel's, by a dialectic of moment and englobing whole of experience. But whereas before transcendental philosophy came into its own, the problem confronting ontology was often one of proving the existence of the infinite ground, the difficulty is how to protect the moment from absorption into the All, conceived as horizons, in relation to which the moment finds its sense.[1]

As I—the reflecting observer—am, according to Merleau-Ponty, but a fold in Being, a reprise of possibility founded in Being and Being-founding, whose actuality consists entirely in the present initiative's crystallization of a figure, it is clear that Being can only appear, and I can only be, through my actually existing: *Being is act.* This realization mesmerized Sartre, but Merleau-Ponty adds that none of those acts through which Being comes to be and to possess itself can ever achieve full clarity and self-possession. Each is but a partial and momentary conquest, a point of view incapable by definition of ever totally overcoming the inertia of the All. Hence the "contingency of the good." Every accomplishment is provisional, and accumulation can only be effective (again as Sartre says) through the renewing, creative, miraculous act of reprise which perpetuates horizons around a figure. Hence, too, the menace of a *rechute dans l'être,* of reverting into Brute Being—is never exorcised. The death of the individual is but one of the forms in which the inertia of matter overcomes the energetic initiative of an Ego; the complex is another. The energy of the sub-

---

1. The problem has already found its transcendental form in Descartes' *Méditations,* where it becomes very difficult to understand the status of finite substances. This is not to suggest that the Thomistic "analogy of being" is without its mysteries, too; but there is no doubt that St. Thomas never questions the existence of individual sensible material things and that the problem for Thomists remains to make the ascent from these things to the infinite *esse* convincing.

jective center cannot overcome the paralyzing drag of a past figure, and the present figure is unable to maintain in the margins what normally would be sent to its place in history; thus a whole life gets stuck in the form of one of its moments. Similarly, hallucinations are a failure of the corps propre to take in hand its own forces. *The Structure of Behavior,* referring to the inertia of instinctive structures, terms the relative incapacity of lower comportments to command their world "getting stuck in the stimulus."

This is not to say, with Sartre, that the moment is entirely creative or even that it must ever be instantly re-created. Granting that without a present act of reprise—the "founding act"—there would be no structured history, no body, no things, it must nevertheless be understood that the sense-giving, future-opening, figure-forming moment does not create the past, the body, the other people and things, but depends on them itself. The sense-giving act, centripetal as well as centrifugal, is a reprise that espouses what is offered interior to its horizons as solicitations, as intentions precisely for its *prise,* and as guiding resistances. One must not underestimate the reality of the past, of things, the possibility of accumulating an *acquis,* or the future-engaging power of the corps propre's structures.

It is, however, this recognition of the instant's opacity and the attempt to give it, through the device of the corps propre, a solidity transcending the Ego's activity that creates the central difficulty. To explain how these solicitations and resistances can be relevant to a genuinely creative center of initiative, Merleau-Ponty makes the proffered intentions and the reprise both moments of the same totality—Being itself. Indeed, when the reprise is regarded as a fold in Being, the subject primordially conceived as corps propre is scarcely distinguishable from its objects and from its world. The primitive and the child lack the civilized adult's sense of where the inner and the outer worlds begin and end; the commonsense adult considers en soi most of the configurations the philosopher has been able to recognize as narrowly dependent on existential acts. Indeed, the commonsense man tends to objectivize most things, modern philosophy to subjectivize them. Recognizing a search for Being in both unifying tendencies, the phenomenologist affirms both horns of the empiricist-idealist dilemma as constituent elements in a dia-

lectic within Being itself. But in overcoming the traditional opposition of subject and object through merging both in the moment of
consciousness, the existential phenomenologist's meditation, as we
suggested a moment ago, achieves such an ontological unity that it
sometimes seems that, despite the fact that every figure is the result
of the historical initiatives of Ego, the Ego itself is nothing but the
accumulation of the results of such acts sedimented as nature and
second nature. The status of the individual moment—which as both
result and cause seems dissolved in a circle—is as paradoxical as it
was for Hegel.

Thus, despite all that Merleau-Ponty has done with the notion of the
corps propre to render credible, in contrast to Sartre, the incarnation
of existence, nevertheless, at precisely the moment of the transcendental viewpoint's triumph—that instant when it grasps Being, ap-
prehending *das Sein* in the *Seienden,* when it sees all of history implicit in the moment, all of nature in the thing, and the person as
ground of the thing—Merleau-Ponty still claims an almost vertiginous
importance for the prereflective act which founds the world! One is
left with the impression that the very realization of this insight will
break the spell. The mere touch of such a transcendental awareness
seems to "dismember the field," tearing in the tense web of lived
time a breach through which "the substantiality of things will pour
out" and matter disintegrate.[2] In any case, the activity of life, consciousness, Ego, tends in such a philosophy to take on absolute
value, and existentialism's temptation to activism and negation of all
anchorage is not an aberration invented by Sartre but is rooted in the
implications of the transcendental viewpoint. The problem is already
before us clearly in Hegel's *Logic*.[3]

2. "If there is not an interminable doubt and 'je pense,' it is because I
throw myself into temporary thoughts (*des pensées provisoires*) and by the
very fact surmount the discontinuities of time" *PP,* pp. 456–57. The working
notes published by C. Lefort along with the uncompleted text of *The Visible
and the Invisible* are frequently preoccupied with this problem, in the form
of the difficulty that philosophy must speak, yet what is cannot really be said.
"Comment toute Φ [philosophie] est langage et consiste cependant à retrouver
le silence" *VI,* p. 267.

3. In reading Hegel the problem always is to understand the status of
the *Gestalten,* the ambiguity of which is supremely and deliberately main-

How grave the problem is grows clearer and clearer in the last essays. Despite the avowed opposition to Sartre, despite the obvious effort to awaken a feeling for the need to respect Being and avoid activism, indeed precisely because of the breathlessness with which the endeavor is carried out, the weights and balances intended to maintain the dynamic, ever-widening circle of Merleau-Ponty's reflection in equilibrium have not successfully halted the tendency to reduce all structure to *sens*. Precise points to urge against such a construction are hard to discover in Merleau-Ponty's text, for the distinctions so confidently relied upon in common experience have all been reduced or bracketed: can the phenomena they expressed, the everyday experience they described, the structures they symbolized be accounted for satisfactorily by a philosophy in which the existent is a fold in Being? If one's body knows things as "an annex or a prolonging of himself, encrusted in his flesh," for whom "the world is made of the body's very own stuff" (*TM*, p. 197), it becomes very difficult, indeed veritable nonsense, to want to distinguish effectively (and not just in principle) the deepest elements in the cultural environment from the natural, simply historical acquisitions of the body, from the *historicité primordiale* which would be the givenness of the body's own structure. It is virtually impossible to separate the elements in a painting that are due to the painter from those due to the things, or in things seen the *texture imaginaire qui les tapisse* from the real which is thus filled out, or, for that matter, me from that Other who haunts me in the fascination of our being together—for in the final analysis, according to Merleau-Ponty, we haunt together *un seul être actuel* (*TM*, pp. 195, 199).

This blurring of distinctions is based in another difficulty: Everything in this philosophy of le corps propre is reduced to the existential and to the historical accumulation of the results of existential acts. But that accumulation itself is effective only to the extent the present

---

tained by that Hegelian word par excellence, *Aufheben*. Why it cannot be otherwise, why transcendental philosophy will inevitably fall into this ambiguity so long as it retains its anti-objectivism is something we are seeking to explain in this chapter. On the form the problem takes in Hegel, see the chapter on him in Gilson, Langan, and Maurer, *Recent Philosophy*.

act succeeds in taking it in hand, and since its finitude permits it to do so only with partial success, the effectiveness of a tradition resides partly in our decision to "play the game," not to break the spell critically, to throw ourselves into the "as if" of a merely presumptive unity. It is disturbing to have to admit that one cannot presume to be simply anything without hypocrisy or to know anything without its ultimately slipping through the limits imposed on it in order to grasp it and to recognize that the only possession of truth that can be considered a success is the application of an idea in practice which will be proven adequate to the always restricted situation by its success in surviving the future. Indeed, the critique of reason is consummated!

Such realizations are disturbing, to be sure, insufficient perhaps for the secure life we believe we might like to lead and fatal to all belief in the objectivity of any structures, but what if that is the way things are? If common sense can be only superficially correct in its belief in the objectivity of things and its own ability to know real natures on which right action can be based, it can provide only a practical form of appropriate truth in certain situations; truth's limits would be established, as Max Scheler points out, by acts of valuating, whose ground lies in fundamental given drives (*Triebe*); it would thus be valid only so long as it is livable. Contemporary physics comes to seem closer to the truth than common experience. The *Phenomenology* has already explained why and how common sense had gone too far, erecting its practical belief into a metaphysics of reality en soi. Merleau-Ponty's critique, like Kant's, would bring it back into its proper, i.e. practical, bounds by indicating that belief in the objectivity of things is simply a matter of hiding the contingency of our encounter with the world under the results of higher acts, of residing securely in the familiar without inquiring into what it is that really grounds it.

At least it is toward this conclusion that the transcendental viewpoint seems to be tending, but perhaps the best reason for refusing to capitulate too readily is the fact that Merleau-Ponty himself, from the first to the last, sees and attempts to resist the dangers inherent in such a position. His descriptions of the otherness of things, essences, ideas and his explanations of their necessity always aim at one and the same time to do justice to the full range of their appearances (thereby accounting for what is legitimate in commonsense experience) and to reveal the lived nature of our experiences of them, thus inviting us always to seek, beyond the visible, the incomprehensible *fond*, the invisible, the brute Being that is revealing itself to us through its myriad faces (*VI*, p. 300). Since he realizes that his terms must express the lived nature of the intentional process even as they deal with moments within this lived All that present themselves as discrete, temporally limited, and in some sense necessary, he must search for new expressions capable of describing a kind of dynamic structure but unburdened with the *en soi* feeling of traditional notions. For example, in a working note dated December 1959, Merleau-Ponty writes: "A world = an organized ensemble, which is *clos*, but which, strangely, is representative of all the rest, possesses symbols, its own equivalences for all that is not it. Painting is this way for space, for instance. . . . Replace the notions of concept, idea, spirit, representation by the notions of *dimensions* [Merleau-Ponty's italics], articulation, *niveau*, hinges (*charnières*), pivots, configuration" (*VI*, p. 277). The text goes on to indicate that the principal starting point is a critique of the usual conception of the thing and its properties and of all positive signification, which should be replaced by the notion of signification *comme écart*, as deviation from a norm. Thus the question becomes, To what extent is the "passage to a superior dimension" prepared in the "given structure"?

When we survey some of the terms Merleau-Ponty has used to describe the thing, we must admit that they do suceed in expressing the experienced fact that each thing has a certain weight of its own but is nevertheless interpretable precisely as an experienced aspect belonging to a broader world than that outlined solely by its own gestalt. For instance, we are told that the thing, once the spell of familiar usage has been broken, becomes a "center of resistance" and "hostile," that one thing is incompossible with another (*PP*, p. 374), and that any thing contrasts to the product of the imagination—whether *Kunstwerk* or hallucination—by its richness and inexhaustibility (*S*, p. 228). In the same spirit, we are reminded that all aspects of a thing, no matter how they are reported, are synonymous (*PP*, p. 374) and that as they unfold in time, they reveal a unity of style. The remark, "The definition of the thing requires the whole subject" (*PP*, p. 373), suggests again the object's inexhaustibility as well as consistency, while the warning, "Its sense is indistinguishable from the total appearance," indicates that its density, its opaqueness, cannot be captured in any of the many clear ideas that can be formed by fixing its aspects. Finally, the feeling of the thing's reality is communicated by describing it as having an activity of its own: it radiates; it is likened to a comportment; its characteristics are presented as living and as anthropomorphic; we are told that it speaks a language of its own, that it has a rhythm of its own (*PP*, p. 373), and, last but not least, that it *écorche notre regard* (*PP*, p. 99)—scratches our attention.

Many descriptions of the thing, however, emphasize more frankly the perceptive activity in their constitution. "The thing and the world exist only as lived by me, or by subjects like me, as they are the chain of our perspectives, but they transcend all the perspectives because the chain is temporal and unfinished. It seems to me that the world lives outside of me, the way absent landscapes continue to live beyond my visual field and the way my past was lived formerly *en deçà de mon présent*" (*S*, p. 228). Again, "A thing is not effectively *given* in the perception, it is *reprise* interiorly by us, reconstituted, lived by us insofar as it is bound to a world the fundamental structures of which we carry with us and of which the thing is only one of the possible concretions" (*PP*, p. 385). Those structures of the world we carry with us are recognizably *le montage universel*, given with the corps propre itself, "*une typique* [the general schema as perceived in a typical example] of all the perceptive developments and all the intersensorial correspondences beyond the segment of world which we are effectively perceiving" (*PP*, p. 377).

Once one grasps the sense of the innovation which consists in replacing the transcendental Ego by the corps propre, the ease with which most of the more objective-sounding descriptions can be interpreted transcendentally is the measure of their success as expressions capable of leading one past the structures to that of which they are structures, the fond, "brute Being" as lived by the body. The thing is then seen as hostile and resisting to the willful initiatives of the individual Ego, but what is this hostility and resistance if not the adversity of the weight of past sedimentations in the corps propre? By this realistic-sounding affirmation, Merleau-Ponty is thus merely re-stating, in the noematic mode, that every genuinely creative project must succeed in decentering and recentering the whole natural-cultural organ (the corps propre) in which it will incarnate its novel extension of sense. The declaration that one thing is incompossible with another is no more realistic than the previous statement; it means that when a certain organization of stimuli, grouped in the corps propre, solicits our attention so that we proceed to the formation of a configuration to embrace them, the figure can exist as separate moment in the dynamic world of our experience only by "pushing all other possible aspects of the world to the horizons"; with all of these possible aspects, it remains in close liaison, for it is a figure in the world, a moment of it equivalent to any other; the substitution of another figure for this one is already solicited from the fond while I am attending to the presently formed figure, which can persist only so long as all other possibilities remain merely implicit, for its whole reality consists in this holding-off achievement of the attention. One of the interesting aspects of the painting is its effort to get many things to yield some of their insistence, thus making compossible what is not compossible in normal perception.

Such considerations force one to be aware of the purely existential nature of perception and of the durational nature of its dimensions in Merleau-Ponty's philosophy. The characteristics of inexhaustibility, intersensorial richness, and synonymity are all explicable for him in terms of the dense but consistent stuff of the corps propre out of the depths of whose experience the figure is formed. The comportment-like activity of a thing, with anthropomorphic predicates and its own language, are understandable when we recognize that the thing is formed out of our experience of it.

The statement in *Signs* that the things "snatch at the look with their edges [*arêtes*]" (*PP*, p. 379) might seem more realistic than any of the above descriptions if the same passage did not immediately explain the nature of those arêtes: the articulation of Being, which is accomplished through man (*la jointure et membrure de l'Etre, qui s'accomplit à travers l'homme*), which is to say that these very "edges" are contributed by the intersection of montages of the corps propre. Hence, we are further told, there are no questions of form but only of configuration.

Despite Merleau-Ponty's efforts to salvage a feeling of solidity by speaking of a *fond de nature inhumaine* and of things manifesting "univocal forms and emplacements" (*S*, p. 228), radiating sets of stimuli which receive their consistency from the source, his philosophy systematically tends to present the moment as part of a living whole, to see the figure as supported by a lived *fond*, to consider the thing as a correlate of the general *montages du corps propre* as *typique de l'Etre*, rather than to seek out its atypical qualities. The idea of Renoir looking at the sea to discover the stream in *"Les Lavandières"* elates Merleau-Ponty: the artist is indifferent to what may be peculiar to this stream, as he seeks instead *la typique de l'eau*, indeed an imaged *fond* expressing Being itself, much in the spirit of the images gathered by G. Bachelard in *L'Eau et le rêve*. Not the absolute otherness—the *Selbstständigkeit*—of the individual and of the particular structure but the thing in general is always presented as what is really interesting (*PP*, p. 373). It is as though all figures that succeed in winning for themselves a certain space and sufficient endurance to make recuperation of Being possible were equivalent instances of a whole, and the possibility of polarizing that whole were the only interesting problem. Projected on the moral plane, this partially explains the sense of helplessness that creeps into certain passages of the "Practica"—a feeling reinforced by Merleau-Ponty's own silence on political matters during his last years.[4]

Sartre's claim that Merleau-Ponty came to feel acutely the impossibility of moving the massive weight of history through the fragile word might have resulted from the invitation, presented throughout his philosophy, to direct his regard past the individual, past even the class, directly to the whole of social being itself. This view of things as elements in a field—surely a permanent feature of all future transcendental philosophies—invites the movement to the largest possible horizons, those of experience itself, i.e. *de l'Etre*, in the sense in which it figures in Merleau-Ponty's philosophy. If, however, nothing halted the transcendental movement of the regard, if our *champ*, most authentically attended to, had only the whole of history, the global situation, and humanity as such as its *fond*, if every action had to be considered for its eternal reverberations, and if the

---

4. The indifference never reaches the point of hostility, as in Hegel, but then Hegel, in characterizing the *begrifflose blinde Mannigfaltigkeit der Natur* as Nature's *Ohnmacht*, is perhaps only being more *Konsequent*. Cf. *Wissenschaft der Logik* (Lasson), 2, 247.

cariatide du vide had to bear with its every act the whole of Being on its shoulders, action would indeed be paralyzed. But this obvious overstatement reveals merely the tendency or underlying tension within transcendental philosophy, for existence is possible, after all. Merleau-Ponty repeatedly reminds us that there is something rather than nothing, provided only that we manage in fact to take our life in hand and go ahead and live it. The corps propre, despite the fact that it itself has no ends to offer (and that is a problem), will, when directed by practical intentions discovered in real lived situations, continue to furnish manageable configurations. It is only when the things which appear in the course of daily living are reflected upon, turned into ideas, making of their engaged configurations disengaged eternal possessions of the truth—explanations, as "L'Homme et l'adversité" disapprovingly puts it—that the antinomies of the dialectica confront us and the reality of the things tends to slip through our fingers.

But there is good reason to think that even practical existence is not that spontaneous. Action itself requires some reflection; we are always under pressure to stake out a future reaching farther than the spontaneous synthesis "worked in immediate presence of the thing" under the guidance of the practical projects of the shortest range. The situation itself pushes men to seek in things some unequivocal objective guides as they attempt to base their actions on real structures which reveal an already-engaged and intelligible future, manifesting sufficient distinctness to be comprehensible and hence dependable and sufficient clarity to provide a limited element of absoluteness, at least to the extent of a modest, circumscribed something which is what it is.

Can such necessity, finite in comprehension but absolute within its limits, be discovered within our experience? Or is Merleau-Ponty correct in assuming that the most elementary grasp of the field theory of perception suffices to inform common sense that der Traum of objectivity ist ausgeträumt, that we must awaken from the dream of objectivity?

Leibniz's declaration that the only sure way to refute a theory in philosophy is to replace it is applicable here, but to confront the problems raised by Merleau-Ponty's version of transcendental philosophy and then to seek to integrate the evidence of "constitution," which led to the historicizing of the thing, into a description in which there would also be a place for the evidence that not everything can or should be historicized, in the process discovering the lacunae in the realistic theories that led to the thing's dissipation,[5] would be a vast undertaking out of scale with a concluding chapter. It would require a detailed analysis of the effort to mathematicize the thing (the history of which, from Galileo to Kant, has already been superbly developed by Heidegger in his 1936 Freiburg *Vorlesungen*, published in 1964 as *Die Frage nach dem Ding*[6]) with a critique to show where it rejoins and where it ignores the full range of common experience (totally—and disappointingly—lacking in Heidegger's book, because of difficulties we shall suggest at the end of this chapter). Furthermore, the history of art and literature would have to be examined for evidence of the role of things serving as a typique much more finely and more objectively structured than the very general typique provided by the perceiving body's montages—an inquiry that should focus on the extent to which and the exact way in which the arts have been modeled on these various sorts of given structures and the exact extent to which they have really declared their independence from them by fashioning structures of their own. Vague suggestions about *les épures de l'être* and la typique would then have to be surpassed in a direction suggested by precise historical evidence. Finally, one would have to undertake a most difficult inquiry to show in detail what we learn about our own givenness from the way things are given; in that study the things would be interrogated not as mirrors of God or of men, but (and here the Copernican revolution would be truly reversed) as *Anstösse* truly relevant to us, because both similar and different, if we too are a kind of thing, higher than material objects and animals.

5. Max Scheler's thesis that this is caused by a change in fundamental ends, from contemplation to *Beherrschen,* is undoubtedly true as far as it goes but gives only one side of the story. Inadequacies in the realistic formulations of the high Middle Ages are surely also to be blamed, just as the same inadequacies today keep neo-Thomism from imposing itself. In Scheler's position see the two long works grouped together in Band 8 of the Works, under the common title, *Die Wissensformen und die Gesellschaft.*

6. M. Heidegger, *Die frage nach dem Ding* (Tübingen, Niemeyer, 1962), pp. 42–100.

To raise our questions concerning the figure and fond analysis, we may turn to Merleau-Ponty's working notes from the period preceding his death, which were published with *The Visible and the Invisible*. They reveal Merleau-Ponty's continued preoccupation with the problem that, from the viewpoint of his most mature reflection and in the terminology of the last years, he himself would call the problem of structure and essence. Having responded to the ancient dualism aporia with a philosophy of Being lived as *la chair*—leading to the conclusion that "everything in us is cultural (our *Lebenswelt* 'subjective,' our perception cultural-historic) and everything in us is natural (even the cultural rests on the polymorphism of *l'être sauvage*)" (*VI*, p. 307) —he seems prepared to assume the burden of accounting for what strikes common sense as necessary, structured, other, in those dynamic terms, a task that tends to reduce necessity to the sedimented history of a contingent being, structure to the dialectical line between noesis and noema, and otherness to merely a different side of one and the same Being.

In one of those last fragments, he writes:

> Oppose to Sartre a philosophy of structure for which, in truth, contact with geography would be a better formation than contact with history. . . . For history is too immediately linked to individual praxis, to interiority, it hides its thickness too much, its flesh, so that it is too easy to reintroduce into it the personalistic philosophy. . . . On the contrary, geography—or rather the Earth as *Ur-Arche*—brings out the carnal *Urhistorie* (Husserl—*Umsturz*). The question is to grasp the *nexus*—neither "historic" nor "geographic"—of history and transcendental geography, this same time which is space, this same space which is time, which I shall have found by my analysis of the visible and of the flesh, the simultaneous *Urstiftung* [fundamental founding] of time and space, which makes it possible for there to be a historic landscape and an almost geographic inscription of history. (*VI*, p. 312)

The text ends with a cryptic point of the finger directly at the central problem this solution raises: "*Problème fondamental: la sédimentation et la réactivation.*"

But is the problem one of recognizing that sedimentation has taken place, that a sense has been accumulated, that the figure-structuring acts of men have woven themselves into the very perceptual fabric of our world? Or is it rather that there could be any sense to sediment in the first place? Even if the philosopher places the Urstiftung far back in an archaic period, buried under thick layers of cultural sediment and so metamorphized by the intervening events as to be indistinguishable from all but the most recent, the most individual acts, thus relieving us from wondering about the initial encounter, the primordial *déhiscence de l'Etre,* how can we help asking what it was that was perceived in that first bending back of one moment of Being upon another; i.e. how that perceived facet—the Otherness within Being—presented itself to the perceiving part; in short, in what that Otherness consisted phenomenally?

The last notes reveal the philosopher repeatedly trying to imagine this Urstiftung. Clearly he sees that even in the present moment the phenomenon of the opening of the world is being lived and that in the present act of perception the whole mystery is again intact; in my body, in your body, in our body is lived at each instant the mystery of the *écart,* of the separation within Being which permits a space for reflection, the perceptive grasp of a part of Being which is other than the perceiving organ itself (*VI,* pp. 309, 241). The facts that I feel a front and a back to my body, that it has an inside and an outside, that I can touch my hand while it in turn is touching something else, are *Urphänomene.* How then in these primordial experiences of the *percipi* which is Being does the Other element, the perceived, the resisting, the impenetrable present itself? Is it enough to describe the threading of this fundamental givenness in all its fine articulation through all our cultural acts merely as "nervures," as "arêtes," as "épures," as the "structure" of Being? This is the central aspect of *le problème fondamental: la sédimentation.*

The words *"essence," "Wesen,"* and "structure" appear frequently in these last notes, and once even approvingly, in the form of Heidegger's notion, *Es west* (*VI,* pp. 228, 260, 280, 309). Often, the remarks are merely criticisms aimed at the pretensions of ideas to "eternal truth," recapitulating points made in *The Phenomenology of Perception,* rather than detailed descriptions of how the phenomenon of essence ought to be interpreted authentically. We are reminded again that only so long as language, in which the aspects of Being get fixed, remains in living contact with brute Being can the word undergo the constant renewal which alone keeps it from freezing into a dead substitute for Being. "Nominalism is right: significations are only *defined separations (écarts définis)" (VI*, p. 291). More positively, we are told that instead of concepts, significations, ideas, we must see structure at work in the self-revelation of Being. *"Décrire la structure, tout est là,* and the integration of structures in the *Sein,* sense as investment (the sense of the word I say to someone crashes upon him, takes a hold of him before he has understood it and snatches an answer from him)" (*VI,* p. 290).

From this it is apparent that the problem of structure is inseparable from the problem of the existence of a world within which there are many consciousnesses, but we recall that in the *Phenomenology* both the problem of the unity of the one world for my many acts of cogito and the problem of its oneness for the many cogitos of other people were solved by exactly the same principle, "generality." Without generality there would be no field; without a field there would be no generality. "There is no longer any problem of the concept, of generality, of the idea once one has understood that the sensible itself is invisible, that yellow is able to set itself up as level or horizon" (*VI,* pp. 273, 290). In other words, even the least sensibilium is not really seen, i.e. grasped en soi independent of the whole sensory system, without implication, simply as that which it is; rather, each moment stands out from the system and thereby implies it, and the very possibility of this standing out is inherent in the system and hence is repeatable to infinity, i.e. general. Each perceived being is "a structure or a system of equivalences about which it arranges itself and of which the flexuous line of the painter or the sweep of his brush is the peremptory evocation. It is a question of this *logos* which silently speaks in each sensible thing, to the extent it varies round about a certain type of message, of which we can get an idea only by carnal participation in its sense, by espousing with our body its manner of signifying." This logos manifests itself, of course, as gestalt pregnant with an always partly invisible sense—that is "the *Etwas* of which the parceled phenomena would be a manifestation" (*VI,* pp. 258, 261).

In this vision the otherness of the thing or even of the *quale* is reduced to such a minimum that one might wonder if it is still objective enough for anything to be said of it. To this objection Merleau-Ponty offers a blunt answer (backed up by the eloquent proof of his own writing): "The *quale* seems opaque, indecipherable, just as life does not inspire the man who is not a writer to say anything. But, on the contrary, the sensible, like life itself, is, for the philosopher (that is to say, the writer), a treasure chest of things to be said. And just as everyone finds true and rediscovers in himself what the writer said about life and its sentiments, so too the phenomenologists are understood and used by those who say philosophy is impossible" (*VI*, pp. 305–06). This note is significantly headed, "Philosophy of the sensible as literature."

Whether one accepts this (in the deepest sense) aesthetic philosophy or not, the challenge it poses has to be met, and it imposes on proponent and opponent alike a very similar task. The proponent's challenge is to carry forward a work Merleau-Ponty was hardly able to begin: From the heights of the transcendental formula of *In-der-Welt-Sein* as *Charnière de l'Etre,* he must descend to the more pedestrian but very difficult business of making sense, one by one, out of the particular appearances of essence, the various strata of nature, the individual *typiques de l'être* which choke the world of daily experience—the varieties of things, the multitude of structures of every and all sorts which furnish the world of busy existence. There is indeed a great deal for philosophy to focus upon, and the whole series of levels Merleau-Ponty passed over in silence are perhaps as eloquent as those for which he sought to offer some description. For every problem to which he made a precious contribution, like that of body-soul, there are inevitably others, like that of the *Selbstständigkeit*—the relative independence—of particular material structures, of otherness, or of objective necessity which are not adequately accounted for either in terms of the sedimentation of a prodigiously long history or merely as dimensions of Being.

On the other hand, one can scarcely object against such a philosophy without accomplishing in one's own way virtually the whole task the proponents of this phenomenology take upon themselves. A replacement for it would entail phenomenological descriptions as far-reaching as those the followers of Merleau-Ponty must take on and as capable of accounting for the existential dimensions of *In-der-Welt-Sein* as for the appearance of objective structure in things. The mere gathering of descriptive data to corroborate realist convictions about the nature of things is not sufficient, for the transcendental philosophers (with Merleau-Ponty in the forefront) have made us realize that there are levels of Being, as real as things and natural essences, which cannot be described at all in objectivist terms. Realistic schemes have encountered difficulty in making a place for creativity and in handling in terms of fixed form such phenomena as the movement of music, the coming-to-be of a painting through the stroke of a brush, the crystallization of a class consciousness through the impact of historical events, or the role of the *mot d'ordre* in precipitating and guiding revolution. Merleau-Ponty's philosophy provides a propaedeutic for learning to live these experiences of intentional Being and a model for espousing their movement through a living expression capable of fixing attention without "freezing vision" or at least of guiding attention past the figure to the uncomprehended fond. If that philosophy finds it difficult to account for the full charge of finely articulated structure, for the future-engaging necessity of the things in our perceptual experience, and even for the possibility of certain finite judgment, so, on the other hand, does traditional objectivist philosophy find it impossible to make an adequate place for *les épures de l'Etre,* for incarnated perception, for the historical-cultural sedimentations, indeed for dynamic finite liberty.

This conflict might lead one to surmise, in the best mode of pessimistic existentialism and à la William James, that one must virtually choose, according to whichever set of phenomena his faith tells him is really important, one of these ways of being-in-the-world and renounce any attempts to deal philosophically with the other. While the problem is grave, however, such a skeptical conclusion does not yet, I hope, seem warranted. It can be adequately answered only by descriptions embracing both the objective and the existential phenomena. This would seem within the power of a perfectly critical phenomenology.

But then there is diversity among phenomenologies. One is tempted to wonder whether this is not simply the result of their being insuffi-

ciently critical, of assuming certain ontological starting points when
it is their task to force all evidence to show its credentials through
radical interrogation of all assumptions. If, however, one considers
the contrasting starting points—the underlying assumptions about
Being which separate two such fundamental ontologists as Merleau-
Ponty and Heidegger—one wonders how there could be any hope of
getting behind starting points that are fundamental to that degree.

The student of Heidegger would criticize Merleau-Ponty for failing
to bring out a fundamental dimension of the problem of Being: on
the one hand, he makes the existence of the present moment of sense
—the figure as figurating—depend too much on the present act of the
Dasein (even though understood as corps propre); while, on the other
hand, he makes it seem as though any present or possible figure lay
implicit in Being from the moment of the initial "explosion of
Being," so that when I speak, or paint, or even gesture, "Being says
what it has always wanted to say." This not only obscures the mystery
of the *Urstiftung,* but fails to face up to the mystery of each authentic
creation's bringing to be something really new out of . . . well, out
of the Nothing, Heidegger says. In contrast, Heidegger deliberately
encourages in every way he can *Gelassenheit,* the active holding oneself open to a possible further revelation on Being's part that will
throw new light on the Urstiftung and on the origin of the new in all
originative thinking.

Though it is true that Merleau-Ponty has not emphasized the
mystery of Being's coming-to-be, he has at least admitted it. He never
presents the original *déhiscence de l'être* as anything but an ultimate
mystery. It does seem, however, that he would reduce the mystery to
the one initial occurrence, the Urstiftung, in which Being first opened
a space in itself, *se creusa,* thus founding once and for all *un sens.* At
one point in those last "working notes," where, writing for himself,
Merleau-Ponty poses problems in a most unguarded fashion, he faces
the issue squarely.

> I bring into doubt the evolutionist perspective. I replace it by a
> cosmology of the visible in this sense that, considering the
> endotime and the endospace [terms invented by Merleau-Ponty
> for the occasion], there is no longer for me any question of

origins, nor of limits, nor of series of events reaching toward a first cause, but [rather] a single explosion of Being once and for all (un seul éclatement d'Être qui est à jamais). (*VI*, p. 318)

This, the Heideggerian would charge, basically commits the Hegelian error, the humanist mistake par excellence: it reduces the mystery of Being to the contingent fact of the corps propre's coming-to-be[7] and consequently accepts something very much like Hegel's notion of necessity (*Notwendigkeit*), in which the need (*Not*) founded by Being's coming-to-be is filled up progressively by a decentering and recentering of the system, rendering explicit what was implicit in the horizons. This may be contrasted with Heidegger's attempt to guard the mystery of the fulfillment of the need, with emphasis on the "grace" of Being's new revelations. For him the mystery is compounded by the fact that each step in the history of Being is an explicitation of some (but by no means all) of the possibilities established at the moment of Being's appearing; and yet each of these new epoch-founding events on Being's way requires a new contribution "from out of the *Nichts*." For Hegel, on the contrary (and in the eyes of the Heideggerian critic Merleau-Ponty in this fundamental perspective resembles Hegel), the *Nichts* of the beginning is not a pure nothing, a genuine transcendent, "but a nothing from out of which something shall come."[8] Because it is of its nature one-sided and therefore structured with a kind of openness, the Something is already mediated by the *Sein* and the *Nichts* of the absolute beginning, of which the Something is only a determination.[9] This moment, this *Etwas,* then, has its sense for Hegel (as it does for Merleau-Ponty) in its ground— in being and the Nothing—and needs the others implied in its one-

7. Bertrand Russell objects somewhere to the notion of the a prioris being the result of a contingent fact. How can that which is the ground of necessity itself depend on a contingency? Merleau-Ponty would answer that the corps propre did not have to happen but, once it did, then things cannot now be otherwise than they appear.

8. See Thomas Langan, *The Meaning of Heidegger* (New York, Columbia University Press, 1959), pp. 94ff.

9. Hegel, *Wiss. der Logik,* ed. Lasson, 1, S. 58.

sidedness in order to be fully intelligible. For Hegel, this *need* requires that the others be formed if the *Etwas'* sense is to be full, i.e. if there is to be knowledge of it in an unqualified sense—in other terms, if the *Sollen* upon which science is based, i.e. the resolution (*Entschluss*) to think thought as thought,[10] is to be fulfilled, thus achieving the *Selbstständigkeit* that is the sign of necessity.

To perceive more clearly how closely Merleau-Ponty's position resembles the Hegelian conception, one need only ask how a given figure may be said to need the potentialities which, while remaining in the background, nevertheless make up its sense. In what way does one given figure call forth a later figuration (or explicitation of its implications)?

Merleau-Ponty has never faced the issue as explicitly as Hegel did in the *Greater Logic*. If each figure is regarded in terms of its origin, it clearly owes something of its existence to those preceding ones, now sedimented in the horizons, which contribute to its sense. But its future—its explicability to infinity—also makes up the depth of the thing figured at the center of attention, and though Merleau-Ponty's term, "motivation," situates the problem of how that series of relevant future figures is called in Being, it does not solve it. In his last notes Merleau-Ponty recognizes that ambiguity covers problems that must be dealt with.

Once one has abandoned the realist solution, which contends that an objective structure existing en soi is somehow able to impose an aspect of itself and thus to motivate anticipations of other aspects according to the sense of the parts revealed by the facet now turned toward the individual, then either the present figure needs the next to fulfill its sense, as Hegel insists, or the recentering must be, as Heidegger proclaims, a mysterious creative act in which a really new element enters the structure, combining with the old to form the sense of a new figure. If the latter is the case, then "the Being of the things that are" (*das Sein des Seienden*) cannot be accounted for by "a single explosion of Being, once and for all," for the Question of

10. "So würden alle weitern Bestimmungen und Entwicklungen nur bestimmiere und reichere Definitionen dieses Absoluten sein" Ibid., S. 59.

Being confronts us rather in every advance of thought. On the other hand, if the Hegelian explanation is accepted, it is difficult to understand how determinism is avoidable. This development was detestable to Merleau-Ponty, but one cannot always force one's philosophy to avoid conclusions to which one's sensibilities respond negatively.

It is perhaps significant that both the last essays and the working notes are concerned not with freedom, but with the self-revelation of Being. The paradox of creativity is expressed but not resolved in one note:

> The amorphous perceptive world of which I spoke *à propos* of painting—perpetual resource for remaking painting—which contains no mode of expression yet calls for and requires all of them and resuscitates with each painter a new effort of expression —this perceptive world is in the final analysis Being in Heidegger's sense which is more than all painting, than every word, than every attitude, and which, grasped by the philosopher in its universality, appears to contain everything that will ever be said, while leaving us to create it (Proust): it is the *logos endiathetos* which calls for the *logos prophorikos. (VI, p. 273)*

Such a text once again situates the problem very well, but does it offer anything to solve it? The very indefinite term, *appeler,* which suggests that Being is actively soliciting the formation of its own sense, still leaves a certain latitude to the *Dasein* to create the precise form it will take. Moreover, the reference to Heidegger can be true only if it is understood to mean that the world presently perceived has in its depths the results of all the past revelations of Being and that the necessity of Being's coming-to-be involves the need that is filled from out of the mysterious *Abgrund* of the Nothing—a conclusion that no text of Merleau-Ponty authorizes.

Nor should the mystery of the coming-to-be of Being, ambiguity, be invoked if it is used to cover up problems that reason can continue to investigate. One must admit the thoroughly mysterious element in the coming-to-be of anything really new, and such newness can be found in the realm of human creativity. Merleau-Ponty would not be happy to hear us claim his theory obscures this point. On the other hand, however, Heidegger's glorification of mystery diverts attention from the extraordinarily stable and finely articulated structure of nature that is accessible in perception and able to guide our action because those structures themselves have engaged some of the future, and thus provide quietly much of the cadre within which the dynamism of history unfolds.

The characteristic reaction of the inveterate Aristotelian realist to all this is not only understandable commonsensically, but motivated by a real problem. He has seen Hegel's attempt to take nature seriously—to integrate its multifarious givenness into his scheme of explanation—produce results that have satisfied no one. Not only are the data twisted to fit the scheme, but, to the extent some positivity remains in resulting descriptions—some givenness that is not thoroughly intentionalized—it seems quite unaccounted for in terms of the ontology revealed by the *Logic.* Husserl, on the other hand, frequently speaks of "material essences," but in the final analysis he explains whatever scientific necessity they may enjoy as due to the "formal essences," which are the a prioris of intentional activity. Heidegger, in *Die Frage nach dem Ding,* does provide a magnificent survey of many facets of the problem of the thing's givenness, but he offers no explanation of how to integrate these structures into his system of interpretation. If the sense in all horizons of interpretation comes from the future-engaging "gift of Being," it is difficult to see what exactly the *Seienden* contribute to the interpreted *Ding,* how this contribution is made, or what sort of necessity it imposes. This problem is clearly felt in the remarkable essay, *"Das Ding."*[11]

The student of phenomenology, replying to this point in the names of Merleau-Ponty and Husserl as well as Heidegger, might suggest that the realist, the supreme victim of uncriticized commonsense presupposition, is looking for what is not there and hence fails to contemplate what is really philosophically significant. He must learn to see beyond the figures which monopolize our daily practical attention to the figurating, for that is where the ultimate essences are to be found. The significant structures, those holding the key to Being's coming-to-be, are those of the *Dasein;* they are the a prioris of the

11. In *Vorträge v. Aufsätze.*

perceiver's *In-der-Welt-Sein*. But the inveterate realist will answer indignantly that once the phenomenologist—in this, just another Kantian—begins interrogating phenomena, the thing is lost. The assumption that the thing is known only as *vorgestellt*, its sense lying in the *vorstellen*, denies from the start all real transcendence on the thing's part. But does the phenomenological procedure, which entails the resolution (Hegel's *Entschluss*)[12] to regard our experience first from the viewpoint of the experiencing, obligatorily eliminate the possibility of accounting for objective structure? Does it perforce tend to dissipate rather than bring out their appearance of otherness?

For my part, I am convinced that although description from the transcendental viewpoint may invite disaster, it does not necessarily lead to it. The worst difficulties can be traced to a hidden (and, I believe, ultimately incorrect) assumption accompanying the phenomenological resolution: the conviction, persisting in the tradition since the *Meditations,* that perception cannot really transcend, i.e. cannot grasp in any critically acceptable sense, a thing in itself. Thus Husserl was convinced that in my actual perception of the present Abschattung of the thing there can be no necessary comprehension of the sense of the thing's structure such that no future perception could ever possibly cause me to rectify the judgment I would make now on the basis of it. Both Husserl and Merleau-Ponty are at pains to point out that the present Abschattung leaving matters open, my actual notion of any thing always faces the possibility of correction by perception of subsequent profiles.

New investigations of perception and a reexamination of perceived necessity might reveal the invalidity of such an assumption by analyzing representative instances of our grasping unshakably and necessarily the sense of a particular "thingly" structure (and hence of a kind of structure as well) in and through perception of a present Abschattung. That, however, is the work of another volume. Here we shall merely note that these investigations must be exercises in constitutive phenomenology. The influence of past experience on the formation of the present Abschattung must be discussed, and the

12. Hegel, *Logik,* S. 54.

grounding of whatever grasp of the sense of a structure is possible on the basis of the present Abschattung must be revealed. I am confident, provided one does not refuse peremptorily to admit the very possibility of the present perception of future-engaging structure, that evidence concerning both *that* and *how* this is possible will be obtained.

Without supporting investigations these assertions are, of course, only unfounded hypotheses. I raise them to suggest in a preliminary way what may be at the roots of the malaise we still feel in glancing back over the whole course of Merleau-Ponty's phenomenological philosophy: the fear that, in the desire to be radically critical, a counterpresumption has been allowed to replace what Merleau-Ponty termed so well *"la présomption en faveur de l'Etre."* Common sense does presume that it knows things in themselves; thus its knowledge is merely presumed to be always consistent. The philosopher should indeed suspend belief in order to investigate the grounds of that presumption. But must he make a counterpresumption involving the judgment that we can in no sense know the things in themselves? Is not his task rather to discover whether, and if so to what extent, we do know, and how (i.e. under what conditions) such knowledge occurs?

Such would be, I submit, the authentically critical attitude. And if one could maintain it, I suppose one could eventually elaborate a view of the world that would differ markedly from any of the phenomenologies (while, like them, revealing the richness and sense of the creative contributions of the *Dasein*); similarly, because it would presume nothing and would work from the experiencing to the experienced, it would differ from all the realisms (while, like them, facing up to the full charge of detailed otherness revealed by nature and rejoining significantly the very implicit convictions of common experience).

In any event, should such a truly critical program be carried out, the debt it would owe to Maurice Merleau-Ponty would be considerable. Not only is he one of the thinkers—with Husserl, Scheler, and Heidegger—who can teach us generally what it means to interrogate phenomena, but his work gives particular indications of how access may be gained to a special *niveau de l'Etre,* that of the structure of perception or, to put it noematically, of *les épures de l'Etre*. In the final analysis, this philosophy, which unfolds with something of the dynamism and *sens* of a great musical composition, will remind us that *In-der-Welt-Sein* possesses its own dialectical structures. It remains the task of another generation to explore how it is that these lived intentional structures give us access to things which move at rhythms altogether foreign to our own.